JOURNEY INTO CONSCIOUSNESS

One Woman's Story of Spiritual Awakening
With Tools to Assist You on Your Own Journey

—

SHELLY WILSON

Journey into Consciousness
By Shelly Wilson
Copyright © 2013 Shelly R. Wilson
www.ShellyRWilson.com
Bluebird House Publications

Cover design and formatting
by Lloyd Matthew Thompson
www.StarfieldPress.com

Shelly R. Wilson
Intuitive Medium ~ Reiki Master ~ Spiritual Teacher
36511 S 4450 Rd
Vinita, OK 74301
(918) 782-4778
www.ShellyRWilson.com
Shelly@ShellyRWilson.com

JOURNEY INTO CONSCIOUSNESS

One Woman's Story of Spiritual Awakening
With Tools to Assist You on Your Own Journey

• CONTENTS •

FOREWORDS 13
TESTIMONIALS...21
INTRODUCTION 29

SECTION ONE
EXISTENCE PRIOR TO MY SPIRITUAL AWAKENING
  1 • MY ENTRY INTO THE EARTH PLANE 37
  2 • INSECURITIES AT A YOUNG AGE 45
  3 • THE BIG MOVE...51
  4 • WHAT'S WRONG WITH ME?...57
  5 • THE REALLY BIG MOVE 63
  6 • STARTING MY OWN FAMILY 69
  7 • WHAT'S WRONG WITH ME NOW? 75
  8 • I STOPPED EXISTING AND STARTED LIVING 81

INTERMISSION 89

SECTION TWO
SPIRITUAL AWAKENING AND SELF-DISCOVERY
  9 • WAKING UP WITH REIKI 95
 10 • FINISHING WHAT I STARTED 107
 11 • TRANSFORMING AT
       THE TRANSFORMATION CONFERENCE 115
 12 • FELLOW TRAVELERS ON THIS JOURNEY 131
 13 • STUCK ON ORBS 145
 14 • AWARENESS IS HEIGHTENED 149
 15 • OFFERING GUIDANCE TO OTHERS............................171
 16 • JOURNEY INTO MEDIUMSHIP......................................183
 17 • JOURNEY INTO MEDIUMSHIP - PART TWO 195
 18 • I AM A REFLECTION OF YOU 211

SECTION THREE
TOOLS TO ASSIST YOU ON YOUR SPIRITUAL JOURNEY
 19 • TEACHING WHAT I KNOW..221
 20 • CHAKRA WORK...241
 21 • MEDITATIONS TO ASSIST YOU 247
 22 • CREATING THE LIFE YOU DESIRE 269

CONCLUSION 279
APPENDIX..283
PERSONAL RECOMMENDATIONS 297
ABOUT SHELLY 301

This book is the story of my journey into consciousness.
It is dedicated to all who are embarking
or continuing on their own spiritual journey.

I am grateful for my family and friends
and ALL of the experiences I have had.
I love you and am so thankful for YOU!
Your presence and support in my life are
appreciated immensely.

I offer you peace.
I offer you love.
I offer you friendship.
I see your beauty.
I hear your need.
I feel your feelings.
My wisdom flows from the Highest Source.
I salute that Source in you.
Let us work together for unity and love.

~ Mahatma Gandhi

Our deepest fear is not that we are inadequate.
Our deepest fear is that we are powerful beyond measure.
It is our light, not our darkness that most frightens us.
We ask ourselves, Who am I to be brilliant,
gorgeous, talented, fabulous?
Actually, who are you NOT to be? You are a child of God.
Your playing small does not serve the world.
There is nothing enlightened about shrinking
so that other people won't feel insecure around you.
We are all meant to shine, as children do.
We were born to make manifest the glory of God
that is within us.
It's not just in some of us; it's in everyone.
And as we let our own light shine,
we unconsciously give other people permission
to do the same.
As we are liberated from our own fear, our presence automatically
liberates others.

~ Marianne Williamson

This little light of mine, I'm gonna let it shine...
let it shine, let it shine, let it shine...

• FOREWORDS •

I HAVE KNOWN SHELLY WILSON since 2009 and in that time I've watched her grow spiritually at an exponential rate. I've remarked on it, and I've sat in awe as I watched her grow from being a student to an important spiritual teacher, medium, and, (even though she doesn't think the term applies to her) psychic. I've observed the changes in her self-confidence and skill levels that took place as she sought out and applied the teachings and wisdom gleaned from studying with internationally known psychics and mediums. I've watched as she resolutely and unwaveringly strived to become the clearest receiver of messages from Spirit that she could possibly be.

What I didn't know about Shelly, until I read this book, were the tremendous obstacles that Shelly had to overcome in her life to get to where she is today. As I turned the pages, my eyes filled with tears of sadness at what she had to endure and then I was overcome with tears of happiness as she overcame every obstacle that was placed in her path. Shelly may have subtitled this book "One Woman's Story of Spiritual Awakening," which it is; but it's also so much more.

At its core, Journey Into Consciousness is a moving personal story of spiritual growth that will no doubt inspire all who read it to follow Shelly's lead and create better lives for themselves.

The 'so much more' is that Shelly doesn't just tell her story: Interspersed within this heart-opening, life-changing story are revelations, quotes, affirmations, and meditations that give "we seekers of a better life" important make-sense tools that we can use to formulate our own plan of action and take control of our destiny.

Whether you are just now putting your first foot forward, or you are already firmly on the path of spiritual growth, this book will facilitate your personal journey into consciousness.

Sherri Cortland, ND
Spiritual Growth Expeditor and Author of *Windows of Opportunity; Raising our Vibrations for the New Age*; and *Spiritual Toolbox* – www.SherriCortland.com

SHELLY HAS GIVEN A VOICE to her *Journey Into Consciousness,* as well as given her readers valuable tools to assist them on their own spiritual journey into consciousness. Shelly is truly a beautiful soul teacher and embodies this truth as quoted by Edward George Bulwer-Lytton: "The best teacher is the one who suggests rather than dogmatizes." She inspires her reader with the wish to teach her/himself.

Anthony Hidalgo
www.AnthonyHidalgo.com

JOURNEY INTO CONSCIOUSNESS IS MORE than a concept of spiritual life—it is both a sharing of one woman's experience through the lens of living out her sacred contract in this lifetime and a guide to doing the same in your own life. We are each given the energies, challenges, and gifts needed to assist us in carrying out the work we are here to accomplish. For those who do so through an awakened state of consciousness, the spiral into our authentic nature takes us deeper with each step.

Following one's guidance can be a risky game to play. It often begins with the simplest nudge to change something in our lives. We may not recognize it as guidance; however, if we allow ourselves to tune in and listen to the messages, somewhere along the way we begin to notice the stakes are higher. No longer is it simply about whether or not to change our diet, instead it becomes about empowering ourselves through a more healthy way of living and being. This in turn clears our energy field while opening a broader channel of Spirit connection.

Committing to this journey of consciousness takes an immense amount of courage and even the tiniest dose of faith. As we continue to practice the art of listening and responding to our guidance, the measure of faith and trust increases with each best choice we make for ourselves in response. There is a validation of being—a standing up within oneself to claim the truth of who we are.

With tools to assist us on this journey, we are able to shift our perspective and see our lives from a Divinely-ordained way of being. There is a recognition of how the events that have played out in our early and later years were each a part of an awakening—an opening into the sacredness of our presence. We are Spirit in human form. Yet, at the very core of ourselves, we are Spirit. And we are gifted with the most extraordinary ability to transcend the physical elements of our lives and move into a state of grace. We can remember ourselves into the knowing that we are always held in the arms of grace. This is an absolute truth, dear friends.

Prior to incarnating, we each agreed to come to this lifetime with a purpose. Too often we seek for that purpose to be something grand. We want to be recognized and supported by others while creating a sense of who we are. Rather, that purpose is to simply BE—to be ourselves, to be present in this moment, to be open to receiving our guidance, to be a channel of grace, love and healing on this planet when we need it most. This and only this is our purpose. It plays out differently for each one of us. Some will be in the spotlight, and others will go about their journey into consciousness through the quietness of their inner being. But make no mistake, dear ones, we are all on this journey together.

I invite you to explore your own life as Shelly did hers throughout the course of this book. Consider the events that occurred within and outside of your own control, and then offer those up to the Universe. If you cannot see how each step along your pathway led you to this place with purpose, ask the open question "What do I not understand about this?" and allow the answers to find you. Know that they will indeed do just that.

In the movie, *We Bought a Zoo*, there is talk of 20 seconds of insane courage. Just 20 seconds. How might your life change with those 20 seconds? There is such courage in opening ourselves to see through the lens of the sacred, in releasing attachment to wanting our life's journey to look and behave in a certain way. Let go of expectations, open to the grace always surrounding you and trust you are held in every possible moment in the cradle of love—these are the elements of comfort and strength that move us through this human life.

Shelly has done a beautiful job relaying her own life events in this way. With each remembering, she opens the dialogue with her own spirit, allowing insights to continue flooding in as the lack of understanding moves gently away. The mystery of being a Divine Being, my friends, is that so often we cannot understand the ways of the Universe. There is a force that moves around and between each of us; continually reorganizing the patterns of energy contained within our perceptions. Shelly's ability to see her life through the eye of a sacred contract no doubt shifted emotions, beliefs and sensations about who she is.

The journey into consciousness is one of both healing and awakening. There is an element of each in Shelly's story. As a spiritual teacher for our time, she goes on to share tools that are simple in nature, but mystical in their power to transform your life. Using her own life experience and the wisdom of her spirit, coupled with a regular spiritual practice, Shelly offers a new way of seeing yourself. There are powerful affirmations, meditations and suggestions for releasing points of stagnancy on your journey.

Journey Into Consciousness is not only one woman's story, but also a powerful tool to assist you in opening your heart, mind and spirit to all that is possible. Shelly is a powerhouse of positive vibrations, spiritual support and encouragement. She has many times held space for me as I take steps along my own journey.

We first met in the fall of 2010, as attendees for Lisa Williams' first mediumship intensive. I know we were destined to meet because it wasn't one of those love-at-first-sight type of connections. In fact, it felt more to me like there was a lack of harmony between us in those first moments. As we returned to our homes across the country and began a small group to practice what we'd learned from Lisa's class, a beautiful soul friendship unfolded, and I felt a tremendous shift in our relationship together. It was indeed beyond anything we could have humanly orchestrated. We had what Shelly refers to as a divine appointment to meet one another.

We can't know what Spirit has in mind for us. There's a quote by Oprah that states, "God has something bigger planned for us than we could ever imagine for ourselves." This has been true for me in several cases, and meeting Shelly is one of them. She has been a catalyst on my own journey into consciousness, although I certainly couldn't see that when we first met.

Journey Into Consciousness is an embodiment of the spiritual journey. As you read through it, allow yourself to feel into what is true for you. Quiet the mind and let your inner voice be your guide. Open yourself to the possibility that your life is so much more than you may have recognized up to this point. There is a sacredness to who you are and how you came to be in this place — at this exact moment, you are exactly where you are meant to be.

We are all in this together, my friends, this beautiful and mystifying journey into consciousness.

Jackie L. Robinson
www.JackieLRobinson.com

*J*OURNEY INTO CONSCIOUSNESS IS THE fascinating story of Shelly Wilson's journey into spiritual enlightenment. Shelly takes the reader on an emotional roller-coaster ride as she vividly recalls the momentous events in her life, beginning with her early childhood years. Shelly courageously bares her soul as she describes the sorrowful incidents that defined her life during a time when she concedes that she merely "existed." It is easy to empathize with Shelly since most of us have experienced similar events in our own lives.

Shelly is a warrior—she never gives up—and this determination allowed her to expand her consciousness and spiritual awareness, so that she could start to "live" and not just "exist." With a lot of hard work and persistence, she re-created herself into the happy and fulfilled spouse, mother, and intuitive medium she is today. And the good news for all of us is that we can learn much from Shelly's journey as we strive to reshape our own lives for the better.

I met Shelly for the first time at the Ozark Mountain Transformation Conference in July 2013, and I was a guest on her radio show in September 2013. I can attest that Shelly is a real, authentic person who takes great joy in her spirituality and who loves to help others achieve their own spiritual enlightenment.

Journey Into Consciousness is not just a great read; it is also a road map for all of us to follow as it describes many of the practical tools that Shelly used to achieve her remarkable transformation. I found this book to be comforting and inspiring, and I know that everyone who reads it will be energized to cast aside their negative emotions and embrace love and compassion for everyone.

Garnet Schulhauser
Author of *Dancing on a Stamp*
www.DancingOnAStamp.com

IN EACH OF OUR LIVES, there comes a time of reckoning—not a reckoning from some separate, higher authority or god, but a reckoning from our*selves*. At one time or another, we are all faced with the cold, naked truth of our own self. Then we must own it.

And it cannot be any other way... unless we are happy and content with no further growth or enlightenment!

To ascend even the tiniest step, we must look at ourselves openly and honestly — both our "Light" and our "Dark."

In *Journey Into Consciousness*, Shelly has provided us with an outstanding illustration of just that. Within these pages, she has boldly exposed herself, offering herself as a living, here-and-now example to us all on just what it takes to... journey into consciousness.

Yet Shelly takes us even further than the story of her own journey; she continues on, suggesting tools and practices that may help shine light on our own unique paths!

Chances are, you are holding this book in your hands because you have been feeling the Heart-tug of this sort of reckoning yourself, and have been drawn to read this — a little cosmic joke on yourself, from yourself!

But here you are, so there is no turning back now! Turn to youself and say, "So long! Nice knowin' ya! I'm beginning a new journey now... And I will never be the same." Then hold a funeral for your old self — this could be the most powerful ritual you have ever performed, communicating your intentions and seriousness to every level of your being.

Behold, the old has passed away — ALL things are now made new!

I wish you many, many blessings on your journey.

Now, heal thyself.

Lloyd Matthew Thompson
Author of *Lightworker: A Call to Authenticity*
and *The Galaxy Healer's Guide*
www.GalaxyEnergy.org

• TESTIMONIALS •

Shelly is a remarkable and gifted woman whose passion in life is to help others understand more about what faces us on our journey, about our loved ones on the other side and also the growth that we have to go through in this physical life that we live. She is a blessing to many.
~ **Lisa Williams**, International Psychic Medium and Teacher, author of *Life Among the Dead* and *The Survival of the Soul*

Shelly's books are life-transforming. I am so appreciative of her friendship, her professionalism, her wisdom and her gifts, which continue to bless me and others every day. Her books and her readings are highly recommended and will cause positively wonderful shifts to occur in your life.
~ **Marie D. Jones**, author of *Destiny vs. Choice: The Scientific and Spiritual Evidence Behind Fate and Free Will*

Shelly has an amazing talent that she shares that takes you on a journey into consciousness. Her gifts and abilities help empower your soul to a new and higher level of spiritual insight. She is truly an angel among us.
~ **Nikki Pattillo**, author of *Children of the Stars: Advice for Parents and Star Children* and *A Spiritual Evolution*

Shelly is one of those rare people who have seen through the illusion of life in the physical, and has dedicated her life to helping mankind awaken to the greater reality through her caring, healing and intuitive counsel.
~ **Guy Steven Needler**, author of *The History of God* and *Beyond the Source - Books 1 & 2*

Shelly Wilson is amazing—one of the most authentic soul beings I know. I am very blessed to have worked with her on some amazing projects. Her compassion and gift to others is insurmountable. It is truly a blessing to be walking the path of awareness with her!
~ **Avianna Castro**

Shelly Wilson has been a huge influence on my personal and professional growth. She always leads from a place of love. Her ability to be 'real' with me and her clients at all times has been a blessing. She is a friend, colleague and mentor.
~ **The Intuitive Messenger - Mitchell Osborn**

Shelly Wilson and I have studied and trained together with James Van Praagh and extensively with Lisa Williams over the past several years. Shelly is not only a fellow colleague, but also a very dear friend of mine. I have personally witnessed her amazing gifts and her healing abilities. She has dedicated her life's mission to helping people live their most authentic life possible!
~ **Robinette Meyer**

Shelly, you have completely changed my life and made me believe in myself! We started off as strangers, and now I cherish you as my family. I am truly blessed to have you in my life. The love and support you have shown me is priceless. Thank you with my whole heart!!
~ **Michelle Kane**

I live in Australia so we have not met personally, yet Shelly has been and continues to be a giving, loving and supportive friend to me. Shelly and I met through Facebook, and we have collaborated on Believe in Believing Blog Talk Radio—a platform where Shelly took her leap of faith as a teacher of spiritual practice.
~ **Ros Clarkson**

I have taken Reiki I, II and Reiki Master classes from Shelly Wilson, and she is an excellent teacher—so calm, peaceful, loving, capable, knowledgeable and FUN! She just glows from the inside out. She is a very powerful healer!
~ **Kathy Galvan**

The absolute BEST things to ever happen in my life are Reiki and Shelly Wilson. There is nothing like living and breathing Reiki and having an awesome Reiki Master to help you along the way.
~ **Erica Brown**

I had the pleasure of taking intuitive classes from Shelly Wilson. I learned techniques from Shelly that gave me an opportunity to raise my vibration, while experiencing personal growth on a deeper spiritual level. Her infinite wisdom is truly a source of inspiration!
~ **Jan Green**

Shelly is a wonderful Reiki Master. Her loving guidance and support will help you with your life path. She is a channel for the purest and most loving energy I have had the pleasure of being present to experience. She is truly a light worker that works from the heart with all of the loving energy you can imagine.

~ **Ronna Armstrong**

Shelly Wilson is one of the most positive people I have ever met. Shelly taught me from Reiki I through Karuna Reiki® Master. I am extremely pleased to say I know this wonderful lady. Her smile is contagious, and she is a genuine healer and intuitive.

~ **Camille Sanford**

Shelly is a great intuitive coach. She is accurate and fast in delivering all messages. Her style is clear and easy to understand. With her guidance, I have made some very big life decisions and am pleased with all the results.

~ **Teresa Larson**

Shelly radiates the essence of pure, true love. During class, Shelly gave me affirmation of something that I have known, but withheld for many years - I am a natural healer. I left this class feeling like a whole new person, both physically and emotionally and with a new purpose in life.

~ **Michelle Bratcher**

I have taken Reiki I and II from Shelly. She encourages her students to use their intuition rather than "by the book," which I found refreshing. The energy that comes off of her is so warm and fuzzy!

~ **Miranda Sutter**

I met Shelly several years ago at a private gathering. I was immediately drawn to her. She has helped me numerous times throughout the most difficult couple of years. She is full of love and light!!

~ Julie Johanson

Shelly has the most generous and compassionate heart—always listening and giving positive loving advice, while reminding us that everything is divinely timed. Shelly always takes the time to consciously and lovingly answer questions. Shelly has been such a positive, encouraging light in my life as well as a friend. I have learned and grown so much since I've met her and for that I'm so grateful.

~ Lisa Bachrach-Zeankowski

Shelly has the most beautiful soul. The first time I met her I knew she was special. Shelly is my Reiki Master. I am honored to have become a Reiki Master under her guidance. She is real and genuine - a true loving spirit. I am blessed to call her teacher and friend.

~ Melanie Gooding

• BOOK COVER SYMBOLISM •

THE ONLY REQUEST I HAD for Lloyd Matthew Thompson when he was designing the cover for this book was that I envisioned the caterpillar, chrysalis, and butterfly metamorphosis. Lloyd's creation and interpretation was: "The green background is for growth. The light shining on it includes the DNA double helix spiral in the background. The caterpillar, chrysalis, and butterfly enlarge ascending upwards to the knowledge of consciousness and metamorphosis. Respectively, the red, green, and purple splashes of color represent the Root, Heart, and Crown chakras, to illustrate ascension."

Upon viewing the image, I recognized green is for growth, but also represents the Heart Chakra, Archangel Raphael, and healing, which is the foundation of this book.

Cover design and formatting
by Lloyd Matthew Thompson
www.StarfieldPress.com

• INTRODUCTION •

THIS BOOK MAY REVOLVE AROUND my story, but within each one of us is a story that is being written each and every day. We are constantly writing the story of our lives based on choices — whether we make these choices ourselves or they are made for us. The directions those choices take us form the foundation for our learning, spiritual growth, and even our happiness. From the moment we breathe that first breath of life to the moment that final breath exits our body, our life story is being written. As we become more aware and mindful of our own personal power, we are better able to make conscious choices, and give ourselves permission to take control of our destiny instead of leaving it up to fate.

Writing books about my own journey into consciousness, particularly this one, is a difficult thing. Like many spiritual teachers, I have given in to that inner calling to express these words on paper for others to read.

The urge to recount my personal journey and the knowledge and wisdom I've gained is incessant, beyond ignorable. I don't know if it's my guides prompting me, or if it is my own inner knowingness or Higher Self that's steering the way, but two things are very clear: (1) There must be something that I've experienced that will assist others on their own journey, or the push wouldn't be so strong; and (2) I have to write my story down, and I am doing that right now.

But where do I start? I know that learning to love and accept myself for who I am and embracing all of my experiences as opportunities for learning and growth have been the catalysts for transformation in my life. I also know that this spiritual journey of mine has strengthened and fortified my soul and psyche so that I know that anything is possible, and that we, human beings, can learn to live the life that we deserve to live.

My particular journey has led me to become an Intuitive Medium, Reiki Master, Spiritual Teacher and Author. As the host of two Blog Talk Radio shows, *The Shelly Wilson Show* and *Journey into Consciousness*, my mission is to assist others on their own journey into consciousness while encouraging them to live an authentic life through awareness and empowerment. As a teacher, I reiterate that the time is now to refrain from simply existing and elect to live life fully without regret. Letting go of the past, living in the present and making conscious choices for the future are the catalysts for positive changes in our lives.

Over the years, I've learned that letting go of fear is a crucial part of spiritual growth, and as a human being, I know that fear is what has held me back and inhibited my ability to write this book for a long time. My personal fears about this recounting of my personal journey into consciousness revolve around the uncertainty of what is safe to share: What will my parents think? What will my husband think? What will my children think? Just how much is enough? As Spirit pushed me to begin writing, I kept coming up with every excuse as to why I should not write this book. The fear became especially strong as it became very clear to me that Spirit wanted—no, *expected* me to share everything that I have.

And so, that is what I am doing. As I do so, I acknowledge that the memories of my experiences are solely my perception—my viewpoint. As I tell my story, I do so with the intention of assisting others in awakening to the truth of who they really are and to help them live the life they desire. I apologize here and now if, as my early memories unravel, I inadvertently cause anyone hurt or pain, but my memories are crucial to the telling of my story, and it was Spirit who showed me which memories to share.

When I asked for guidance on this front, in an instant, a rush of memories flooded me—one right after the other. I realized that they were showing me what I needed to share, what mattered, what was important. The memories I was shown are the pivotal ones that impacted me greatly in my early years. I was shown the memories and choices that molded and shaped me, creating who I am today. By shifting my perceptions, I have freed myself from self-imposed limitations. My past no longer defines me; yet I acknowledge the experiences that have made me the person I am today.

Since we humans function on linear time with clocks and calendars; whereas the Universe operates on Divine time, I needed to convey my story in a make-sense way that would be easy to follow. With this in mind, as my story progresses, I have established some linear dates as a frame of reference to follow as I relate to my journey into consciousness, dividing it into three sections as outlined below:

In Section One of this book, I relate my experiences prior to my spiritual awakening. Each chapter begins with a lesson I have learned and ends with a revelation as well as a message to facilitate your journey.

Section Two begins with my spiritual awakening, which I officially designate as May 1, 2008. I began journaling my spiritual path at that time and have incorporated excerpts from my journals. My objective in chronicling and including these personal "aha" moments of learning and clarity is to assist and support my fellow sojourners. During my journey into consciousness, I have utilized many tools that helped me move forward.

In Section Three, I share the tools and wisdom that helped me the most—those tools that I have found to be straightforward, uncomplicated, and therefore, easily incorporated into our daily lives.

In all three sections, I endeavor to share essential details of my story along with guidance and suggestions received from Spirit to help you move forward on your own personal journey into consciousness, and my primary objectives are as follows:

1) To assist in bringing an understanding of one's life experiences and the consequences of choices made without blaming others
2) To learn to heal from the past through forgiveness and shifting perception
3) To allow ourselves to realize our full potential through empowerment and love

Spirituality is a way of life rather than simply a practice.

And so, let us journey into consciousness together...

• SECTION ONE •

Existence Prior to My Spiritual Awakening

In this section, I relate my experiences prior to my spiritual awakening.

Each chapter begins with a lesson I have learned and ends with a revelation, as well as a message and tool to facilitate your journey.

• 1 •
My Entry Into the Earth Plane

LESSON LEARNED

There are no accidents in my philosophy. Every effect must have its cause. The past is the cause of the present, and the present will be the cause of the future. All these are links in the endless chain stretching from the finite to the infinite. ~ Abraham Lincoln

**My conception was not an accident.
I was intended to be born.**

∞

MY STORY

IN THE BEGINNING, A CHILD was born. I wish I could say that my parents met, fell in love, got married and desired to create a beautiful family. Rather, they dated, consummated and created me. I knew early on that my conception was an accident and not intended to occur. This message was passively conveyed to me repeatedly throughout my childhood and unintentionally imbedded into my brain. My parents were young and presumably didn't realize that there was a possibility that IT could really happen. They were married by a Justice of the Peace in June 1970, and I was born on the 19th day of December in the year 1970 at 4:44pm* as noted on my birth certificate. I am pretty sure they got married because it was considered the "right" thing to do. The underlying societal expectations, especially at that time, dictated that individuals are married in order to fulfill their parental obligations "correctly." As we all know, current trends are different.

My mom had graduated from high school and my dad was in his second year of college when I was born. We lived in a very small town in Kansas. My dad switched colleges, so he could commute and continue his education, and they both worked very hard to make a living.

Both of my parents have several younger siblings, and my arrival into this world designated me the new kid in town in the eyes of my aunts and uncles. I call my mom's parents, Nanny and Pa, and my dad's parents, Grandma and Grandpa. Nanny took care of me while my mom worked until my younger brother came along in 1975 (my youngest brother made his presence known in 1978).

I have many fond memories of spending time at my Nanny and Pa's house throughout my childhood and teenage years. Their home was in the country and had lots of space for the five children who still resided there. It had a basement AND an attic, and I got to explore both freely.

---

*Note: I mention specific times throughout my book. I refer to Doreen Virtue's book *Angel Numbers 101* quite often to interpret the meanings of these particular number sequences. According to this book, the number 444 indicates ~ "There are angels — they're everywhere around you! You are completely loved, supported, and guided by many Heavenly beings, and you have nothing to fear."

Nanny would pack me a picnic lunch, and I could sit in the attic and eat it or sit on the stairway leading down to the basement. I am shaking my head at this preposterous memory of eating in the attic or basement. When I asked Nanny, "What was up with that behavior?" all we could do was laugh. It is funny how these simple moments were reanimated, so freshly in my mind.

A very scary wooden bridge crossed Stranger Creek at the back of their property. I remember walking down the gravelly dirt road with my aunt and uncles just to walk across it. Cars would drive across it as well. Walking across the bridge was scary to me because there were huge gaps between the boards. I was and still am afraid of heights. I could see the water below. With sheer panic, I would tremble and shake, taking one step at a time, gingerly placing my foot very carefully on each of those boards. Once I got to the other side, I would have to do it again to get back to their house. As I am typing this now with a smile on my face, I am actually wondering why I put myself through this torture repeatedly because it was by my own choice each time I did it. Maybe I thought the next time would be easier or I would become braver. I do not know.

I remember visiting Grandpa and Grandma on several occasions. My dad's dad spoke very loudly and was quite gruff, but I knew he had a soft side too. He instilled into my dad a very strong work ethic and was definitely "the man of the house." I remember visiting their house in town before they moved out to the country and pedaling a toy John Deere tractor around on the back patio. Grandma always made something good to eat and would tell my dad that I did not have to clean my plate while I was at her house. I can hear her say right now, "Leave her alone. She's full."

As I stated before, I knew early on that my conception was an accident and not intended to occur. My dad accidentally got my mom pregnant, and I was blamed for ruining their lives even though I wasn't there when I was conceived. I knew I was the reason my parents got married, and there wasn't a thing I could do about it. I carried this guilt around with me until several years ago when I had THE talk with my dad in March 2008 and released everything I had been holding in.

While visiting my dad, I opened up the line of communication with him. Little did I know when I began speaking exactly how much of what I had been bottling up was going to come pouring out. I remember distinctly the expression on his face as the words fell out of my mouth. I said everything that I ever wanted to say, and when I say everything, I mean thirty-seven years of self-perceived unpleasant memories, and I could not stop them. They just kept coming!

I recall the words as if I spoke them yesterday, "Dad, it wasn't my fault I was born. I wasn't there when I was conceived. I didn't ruin your life or mom's life. You made choices and you cannot blame me for them anymore." Wow! These words were freeing and empowering! I continued to convey my truths as I perceived them, one after another. My dad was actually the recipient of what I was feeling towards both of my parents because he was available and appeared to be listening. After speaking my truths, I was completely and utterly exhausted, but I was free from the guilt and the weight I had been carrying with me for so long.

For many years, I wondered what karma I needed to resolve or what lesson I needed to learn for having to endure an oftentimes painful childhood. Since I was perceived as the "problem," I became an outlet for both of my parents. Sadly, I have minimal memories of my childhood and those that I do have are not pleasant ones. Thankfully, most of those unpleasant recollections have left my realm of immediate consciousness, and I have just a few that linger. Ironically, I have an uncanny memory with some particulars, such as phone numbers and people's names. I can actually remember the names of most of my teachers. On the other hand, there are those huge gaps and memory lapses that become apparent when my parents, brothers, husband or children will be telling a story, and I will look at them with wide eyes because I do not remember anything about that experience. In retrospect, I recognize these lapses as a type of coping mechanism.

Painful memories still surface on occasion, and I believe this happens to remind me that my past does not define me nor should I allow it to. As I have grown and matured, I understand and acknowledge that those who wound were wounded as well. I no longer judge them for what they did. Words, once they have been spoken, cannot be taken back. Past experiences cannot be changed, but our perception of them can be.

Please understand that I love my parents immensely and am deeply appreciative of their role in my life. A turning point in our relationship was when they returned a gift to me on my 40th birthday that I had given to them three years prior on Mother's Day and Father's Day, respectively. I presented my mom with the book, *A Mother's Legacy: Your Life Story in Your Own Words* and my dad with the book, *A Father's Legacy: Your Life Story in Your Own Words*. I typed the note, "I hope you take the time to fill this book out. It would make a really nice present for my 40th birthday!" and taped it on the inside of each book. I actually forgot about this gift when they each gave me their version of the book. Both of these books offered me an inside glimpse of their own life experiences from their perspective and are gifts that I will cherish forever.

∞

REVELATION

I know that my conception was not an accident. I understand now that it was necessary for me to have every experience that I have ever had. I know I planned my experiences prior to my incarnation, including selecting my parents.

Honestly, I have often wondered what my life would be like if I had chosen differently and been born to different parents. It does not matter though. I needed to have the experiences I did, so that I can be the person I am today. My parents provided me with important opportunities for learning and growth.

MESSAGE FOR YOUR JOURNEY

Reflecting on your own life experiences, I encourage you to recognize the same for yourself. Choose to acknowledge the memories, whether you deem them pleasant or unpleasant, as opportunities for learning and growth. These experiences do not define you, but have undoubtedly had an impact on who you are today. Allow yourself to acknowledge these experiences, express your gratitude with sincerity for having them, and then honor yourself by moving forward with grace and ease. There is nothing to be gained by blaming anyone for your life's experiences. Take ownership of them and see the blessings within the challenges.

TOOL FOR YOUR JOURNEY

Write down your thoughts, feelings and emotions as you spend time in reflection. Pay attention to bodily sensations as well. Read back through what you have written as you are guided to do so. Verbally express your gratitude when you are ready by saying, "Thank you Universe for all of the experiences I have had. I recognize these experiences to be opportunities for learning and growth."

• 2 •
Insecurities at a Young Age

LESSON LEARNED

The way you treat yourself sets the standard for others.
~ Sonya Friedman

I am beautiful.
My physical body is unique to me.

∞

MY STORY

As long as I can remember, I have always felt different. I was conditioned as a child to mind my manners, not to ask questions, keep my opinions to myself, and do as I was told. These things contributed to my lack of confidence and self-esteem. Much to my confusion, I was often told that I had no common sense. Plus, my last name Ditty was fodder for many jokes by my peers.

I really love to smile, but that wasn't always the case. I

used to be extremely self-conscious of my teeth. These feelings began when I was very young. When I was about four years old, I had to have all but the bottom three teeth capped with silver caps because I had tiny holes in my teeth. I was a colicky baby and had too much acid in my system. I can remember being on the hospital bed and being wheeled into the operating room for the dentist to do the work. My teeth were shiny and silver and not really in fashion in the early 1970s. I have no doubt that they would be "in" right now!

These caps were on my baby teeth, so I was stuck with them until I lost each tooth one-by-one. As you may have guessed, smiling was kept to a minimum and most of my photos show a closed mouth smile.

A significant part of the memories about my teeth include when I was about six years old. I was playing alone on the playground near a swing set at elementary school and was taunted by some of the other children because I had silver caps on all of my teeth. I can see the dress I was wearing and the way my blond hair flipped up on the ends.

The problem with my teeth meant that I seldom smiled and would keep my head tucked down; they made me feel self-conscious, so I tended to be shy. This image continues to surface in my consciousness, and I acknowledge that this little girl will always remain with me as she is a part of who I am.

Had I stayed at one school, I think I might have done a better job moving past the teeth issue, but due to the nature of my dad's job as a civil engineer employed with the government, we moved several times throughout my childhood. I recognize that being the new kid at school on numerous occasions played a contributing role with my confidence issues, and I became the quiet smart kid who liked to read. To fit in with others, I learned to listen and observe. I learned to think before speaking. Although I did have a few friends, I still felt alone most of the time.

Physically speaking, I didn't much care for the color of my eyes or the size of my bottom lip. Reaching puberty, my physical body developed. Although my stature barely reached 5'3", specific body parts took this opportunity to flourish. I became very self-conscious of these physical attributes and still have a difficult time embracing these assets fully. I was and still am embarrassed by some of the looks that I get. To be completely blunt, I am self-conscious of my breasts.

Granted, some women would be delighted with what I dislike. I even joked with my cardiovascular surgeon during a thymectomy consultation about having a plastic surgeon reduce them while I was under. Without even cracking a smile, he said that it would not be a wise decision as they didn't know if the tumor I had in the thymus gland was cancerous or not. *Note: I have written more about that experience in Chapter 7.*

Continuing the topic about the insecurities with my teeth...

When the permanent teeth came in, they were severely discolored. Teeth whitening options were not as readily available like they are now. Even as an adult, my dentist, at the time I first addressed the issue, said that the discoloration was caused by antibiotics that were taken by my mom, or when I was a child, so there wasn't much hope or even a possible resolution. My parents made sure we had regular oral checkups, and I even had the honor of wearing an upper retainer because my teeth weren't that crooked. Based on what I was told, I resolved that there was nothing that could be done about the coloring of my teeth, so I gave up and just accepted the color they were.

Through my early 20s and into my 30s, I would have dreams about my teeth falling out and/or being loose. My thoughts would often go to wanting to have them all pulled and get dentures. Now, looking back, this is completely crazy to even think about such a thing, especially since my teeth were healthy and relatively straight.

Dream interpretations indicate that having dreams about teeth are due to feelings of insecurity and also periods of transition. Oh, how I know this to be true! Little did I know the tooth transition that was in store for me, and it's a transformation that started at a metaphysical conference in Arkansas!

During the Ozark Mountain Transformation Conference in June 2009, I had the honor and privilege to meet singer and actress Helen Reddy who was one of the key-note speakers at the conference. *Note: I have written more about that experience in Chapter 11.*

Helen is now a hypnotherapist and traveled to Arkansas for the conference from Australia. I already had a trip booked to visit Sydney the very next month. I took the opportunity to chat with her about the safety of the city as I would be spending much of the trip sight-seeing on my own. She assured me that the city was extremely safe and to forego any worries I may have. After listening to Helen speak, I was guided to approach her and ask about the possibility of having a private session with her while I was in Sydney. She smiled and wrote down her number, so that I could contact her when I arrived the following month.

Once I arrived in Sydney, I immediately called Helen to get directions for my visit the next day. I followed her instructions precisely by taking a train and then walking the rest of the distance. I was met by her at the door of her apartment. Helen immediately showed me the view from her balcony on the 13th floor overlooking Sydney Harbor, and we spoke at length before starting the session. During our chat, I told her that my friend since 6th grade thought I had gotten very strange since I had become spiritual. Her remark was "Perhaps dear, you need new friends."

Then, we began the session. I was lying on her bed covered up with an afghan she knitted for her son when he was young as she guided me through the hypnotherapy session. The session ended when I heard a strange sound outside the window. When I asked what that sound was, she said, "That's a laughing jackass—a Kookaburra. Do you wish to continue?" I laughed and said, "No, this is the perfect way to end the session."

I then sat up and began speaking with her. Helen sternly but lovingly, told me that I needed to have my teeth professionally cleaned. I didn't get upset, but told her that I do go to the dentist on a regular basis and that this was just the color of my teeth. She insisted that I do something about it. Rather than getting upset or even defensive, I recognized that she was simply the messenger.

Upon my return home, I went to my six-month checkup scheduled with my dentist and asked the dental hygienist if there was something I could do, and told her why I was asking. She relayed the message to the dentist who then asked why I was insistent, so I told him the entire story involving Helen Reddy. He laughed in disbelief, but said we could try it.

Well, guess what? You know the rest of the story—the whitener worked. I am no longer self-conscious about my teeth, and haven't had any more dreams about my teeth falling out. Instead, I smile from ear to ear even when no one can see me smile.

Viewing my tooth saga from a Higher perspective, I recognize that the hypnotherapy session was healing and imperative in forcing me to recognize issues that were affecting me in this lifetime. Ultimately, the message Helen delivered after my session was the reason I was there.

∞

REVELATION

Reflecting on those years, perhaps I was special rather than different. I chose to only see my perceived imperfections rather than seeing myself as a beautiful, unique and miraculous creation. I will admit that I am still a work-in-progress when recognizing all of my physical attributes as perfect in every way. The facial features I disliked when I was young now happen to be my favorite. Choosing to change my perception, I eventually shifted the energy of how I view my physical body.

MESSAGE FOR YOUR JOURNEY

I invite you to embrace the you that is YOU. Yes, this means all of you, including any perceived imperfections you may have as well. Recognize that there is no one else in the Universe exactly like you. Make the choice to love yourself for who you are - fully and completely. Choose to change your perception of any unpleasant memories and view them as opportunities for learning and growth. Accept your uniqueness and dismiss any perceived flaws or imperfections, because you are perfect just the way you are.

TOOL FOR YOUR JOURNEY

Practice verbally expressing love for YOU. Look in a mirror and tell yourself, "I love you." You can do this in the morning when you are brushing your teeth and combing your hair. It is important for you to mean it. Allow yourself to truly feel the love you have for YOU and embrace this feeling fully. In doing so, you will attract this same love into your life from others because of the Universal Law of Attraction, which is based on the idea that whatever we give a lot of attention to will become part of our lives. In doing so, you are co-creating with the Universe.

• 3 •
The Big Move

LESSON LEARNED

Continuity gives us roots; change gives us branches, letting us stretch and grow and reach new heights. ~ Pauline R. Kezer

**I am a responsible individual
and quite adept at completing tasks.**

∞

MY STORY

WITHOUT A DOUBT, THE MOST significant and profoundly pivotal experience in my life occurred when I was in the fifth grade. I remember the details as if it just occurred yesterday. Even at that age, I could sense that my life was about to change enormously, although I truly had no idea of the magnitude of what was about to unfold.

My mom's birthday was in September, and my dad took her out for dinner and dancing. Turns out (and I only knew this because it was relayed to me a couple of months later) that my mom met a man that evening who would later become my stepdad. I have no doubt that there was an immediate emotional and physical attraction between the two of them. I also have no doubt that this meeting was destined to occur because they are still married 30+ years later. This meeting was ultimately the catalyst of change for my parents as well as for me.

A family trip had been planned during Thanksgiving break to Orlando, Florida. My mom decided not to go and kept my brothers with her. I made the choice to go with my dad and, boy oh boy, did that choice change my life forever. My dad obviously needed someone to talk to, and I was that someone. During the long drive from Oklahoma to Florida, he poured his heart and soul out to me along with every single indiscretion (according to his perception) that my mom was involved in. I'm sure you know where this is going. I was devastated that my mom would hurt my poor pitiful dad in this way. By the time we returned home from the trip, the detest I had for my mom was HUGE. How could she do this to me? How could she do this to my dad? How could she do this to my brothers?

Little did I know that she also had many stories to share with me. Yes, as soon as I unleashed my fury upon her, she took that as an opportunity to share every indiscretion (according to her perception) that my dad was involved in. As a naïve young girl, I was appalled at what I was hearing and the perception I had of my parents was forever changed. Let me remind you that I was not quite eleven years old, and for the most part, lived a pretty sheltered life in rural Oklahoma. My worldly experiences consisted of an occasional family drive-in movie or roller skating on the weekend.

My parents made the mutual decision that it was time for them to divorce and move forward with their lives separately. My mom headed north to find a job and locate a place for us to live. She found both pretty quickly and called the school I attended in Antlers to let them know that I needed to gather up the necessary paperwork for a school transfer and also do the same for my middle brother in Kindergarten. School was about to be let out for Christmas break and, due to some specific reason I cannot recall, they were going to be letting out a day or two early. I can still see myself walking across the school yard to the Kindergarten building and back to my building. I remember being in a daze and telling my friends goodbye knowing that I would probably never see any of them again.

My 11th birthday arrived and then Christmas came. Everything, for all general purposes, appeared normal. I believe that my parents strived for normalcy for my brothers, because they were so young. The boys didn't have the inside information that I did. The day after Christmas, my world changed. The car and moving truck were loaded. We were leaving my dad alone to take care of himself. My new life was about to begin and the responsibilities that I were soon given were substantial.

My mom hadn't worked outside of the home since I was four, and she now needed my help with the household. Although she had a plan and would eventually remarry, she had to get a divorce first. We lived in a duplex in Broken Arrow, Oklahoma. The daycare my youngest brother attended was directly across from where we lived. My middle brother and I walked to school. I learned to cook, clean, and do laundry very quickly. I became independent and responsible in a very short time.

My dad would drive three hours one-way every other weekend to retrieve us for a visit at his home, which meant he was making a six hour drive just to spend time with us (twelve hours total within two days). He would pick us up at 6:00 pm Friday night and return us at 6:00 pm Sunday night. Some weekends, I really wished that I didn't have to go. Looking back, I recognize and appreciate the sacrifice that he made for his children and his attempts at normalcy for us. Undoubtedly, these visitations were tough physically and emotionally as well as financially. He moved to Washington DC for nine months and then eventually took another job in Arizona, so our visits were limited to summers and holidays. Until he moved out of state, there wasn't a weekend that he missed coming to get us.

My mother remarried as soon as the divorce was final, and we moved into my stepdad's house. Shortly thereafter, my stepdad gained sole custody of his three children, thus we become a large instant family quite suddenly. Since I was the oldest, I was also responsible for the younger children. Babysitting for others was my only source of income even though I wasn't paid for babysitting my siblings. This frustrated me profusely because my friend across the street babysat for my step-siblings while we visited my dad and was paid quite well for her time.

My mom took a temporary part-time job at a local Braum's to earn extra money. In reality, she needed a break and those few hours she worked offered her that break. She made enough money to buy milk and a few groceries and bring my stepdad home an ice-cream treat. I admit that I was frustrated by the fact that I was cooking and taking care of everyone, and then he got the reward; although, I don't feel any animosity about that now. However, at the time, I did feel like I got the "short end of the stick" in regards to that matter.

To this day, I can still see the mounds of laundry piled up in the utility room. Laundry was a daily chore with eight people living in the house. I attempted, typically to no avail, to enlist the younger ones to help me fold the clothes to keep it under control. Even now, I do laundry every day although there are only three of us in my home. Never again do I want to see or fold the mound of clothes that I did in my teen years. That said, I did acquire a lot of basic life skills!

∞

REVELATION

Without a doubt, I acquired the skills necessary to maintain my own future household. The responsibilities bestowed upon me were not anything that I could not handle. I became self-sufficient and mastered the ability to take care of myself and others. I learned to cook, clean and do laundry quickly and efficiently. For a period of time, I would often wonder what my life would have been like if things had been different. I now acknowledge, as I have stated before, that I was intended to have every experience that I had.

MESSAGE FOR YOUR JOURNEY

Consider this analogy - Life is a journey and "pit stops" may be necessary. Road construction and detours may inhibit our path when we least expect it. Ultimately, we will arrive at our destination as intended. With that being said, choose to shift your perception of your experiences and embrace the knowledge you attained in the process of having them. Remember, perception is how we view or perceive an experience through our senses. Choose to see the blessings within every experience.

TOOL FOR YOUR JOURNEY

Take a moment to write down the skills and abilities you have acquired throughout the years as well as the manner in which you learned them – how, why, when and from who. Recognize the importance of these particular life experiences and how they have affected you. Allow yourself to release any negative emotions you may have recalled and associated with these skills and abilities.

• 4 •
What's Wrong with Me?

LESSON LEARNED

Health is a state of complete harmony of the body, mind and spirit. When one is free from physical disabilities and mental distractions, the gates of the soul open. ~ B.K.S. Iyengar

I acknowledge that there is nothing wrong with me.

∞

MY STORY

PUBERTY AND ITS ACCOMPANYING HORMONES brought on a few unwelcome health issues. I began having migraine headaches, my hands would shake, and I had a few black out spells. I had always been a healthy kid except for having the mumps when I was a baby and being hospitalized for epiglottitis when I was about seven years old. As an already self-conscious individual, these new issues really wreaked havoc in my life.

The migraine headaches came first. I had issues with taking pills—meaning I had a difficult time swallowing a pill because I would gag, so I would chew up baby aspirin. Yes, I know the idea is ridiculous to think about. I had to quickly get over my issue so I could take the hard stuff— aspirin and ibuprofen. Many times I would try to tough it out and just deal with the pain in my head. For anyone who has experienced a migraine, you will recognize that this is not an easy task to accomplish.

Soon after, my hands began to shake. In the beginning, the shaking wasn't very noticeable. Years later, the shaking became a source of anguish for me. People would ask me why I was nervous and then laugh at me. My hands would shake so much that I had a difficult time holding a fork to eat. While standing in front of the class without a podium giving a presentation, my hands would make the paper I was holding flutter nonstop. This definitely wasn't cool.

The blackouts came next. After one episode when I was fourteen, I was hospitalized for further testing. The irony was that I also had acquired the chicken pox, so I was quarantined during my stay in the hospital. My choir teacher happened to be the wife of my doctor and was formerly a nurse. She came to visit me in the hospital after school one day and, much to my dismay, chose to share with all of my classmates what was wrong with me—the reason for the blackouts. I truly believe that she believed that she was helping me by doing so, but this help backfired in a big way from my perspective. I was teased and taunted by some as well as ostracized by others. They didn't understand; therefore, they opted to bully or avoid me rather than ask. Not once did I have an episode at school. I guess she thought that making everyone aware of the possibility was a good thing.

According to the EEG test, I was having seizures and was given the diagnosis of idiopathic familial epilepsy. I was subsequently placed on the seizure medication,

Dilantin, which meant I was definitely going to have to swallow a pill daily. I had to have blood tests done regularly to check the dosage. It seemed to me that it was a bi-weekly or monthly occurrence. I didn't have an issue with needles. It was just a nuisance to have this done. I do not ever remember actually having what I would deem a seizure. I only remember having what I would call a black out and could feel when one was about to occur. The first time it happened, I headed straight for the bathroom after meekly calling for my mom. The room was spinning, and it felt like I was heading nowhere fast. I could see what looked like stars in the vast darkness and then I was gone in a flash. I would then hit the floor in a crumpled mess. Although I would be out for just a short amount of time, it seemed much longer on my end. I can remember the look on my mom's face when I opened my eyes after the first time it happened. I'm pretty sure she was scared and didn't know what to do. I quickly learned to recognize when one was about to happen and prepare myself physically in order to avoid the crash to the floor.

I outgrew the blackouts and was able to discontinue the Dilantin when I was eighteen. The migraines, on the other hand, continued until I was in my late 20s. They were debilitating to the point that I would have put myself to bed to sleep them off. The tremors continued to be a source of anguish for me as they became more pronounced. I went to several neurologists seeking treatment and all would prescribe medication, but nothing eliminated them from occurring. More often than not, the side effects of the prescribed medication caused even greater issues than what I was already dealing with. When I was thirty years old, I finally visited a clinic in Kansas City that specialized in tremors. My official diagnosis was essential tremor. Receiving this diagnosis, I also got the prescription of "deal with it." There isn't a remedy for this concern.

Offering you a health update, I no longer take

medication of any kind for any reason. I have had one or two "almost" black outs in the past few years, but instinctively knew what to do and breathed through each incident fully aware and conscious of what was happening. The migraines are a rare occurrence, and I immediately head to bed to rest when they do happen. My hands do still shake minimally, but they are no longer a source of anguish.

∞

REVELATION

I recognize now exactly what was going on with me at the time. The blackout episodes were what I lovingly refer to as "time outs." The migraines and tremors were due to me channeling energy and not having the knowledge to control it and/or release it. As I began working with the Reiki energy, I was able to recognize all of this.

MESSAGE FOR YOUR JOURNEY

Noting any health issues you may have had or are currently having, I invite you to see beyond the issue. Consider the possibility that this may be a clear indication that you may need to slow down, take a break, rest and take care of yourself. As you tune into what your body is telling you, allow yourself to listen to the guidance you receive and take note of it. Honor yourself and what you are feeling. Please remember to seek medical treatment from a trusted physician and do not try to self-diagnose.

TOOL FOR YOUR JOURNEY

Take a moment to write down any concerns you may be having physically, mentally and emotionally with your health. Allow yourself to honor what you are feeling. Recognize that factors, such as stress and financial worry as well as caring for others, may impact your health. Be mindful of what you are consuming. In addition, assess the individuals and their role in your life to see how these relationships may affect your overall well-being.

• 5 •
The Really Big Move

LESSON LEARNED

*We all have big changes in our lives that are
more or less a second chance.* ~ Harrison Ford

**I acknowledge that the chain of events played out
precisely as it was intended to.**

∞

MY STORY

I THOUGHT THE RELOCATION WHEN I was
eleven was a big one. Not so much! The really big move
occurred when my mom and stepdad made the executive
decision to move from Bixby, Oklahoma to Big Cabin,
Oklahoma (a mere 70 miles although it seemed much
farther) just a month prior to my sixteenth birthday. Before
I share this story, I need to give you a little bit of
background and then explain the events leading up to this

move.

Background: Our leisure activities were always centered around the lake—camping, fishing and all activities involving our boat. The weekends that I didn't visit my dad in southeast Oklahoma were often spent camping at one of the two area lakes. We would load up on Friday night and camp until Sunday night. I would like to declare that I really didn't enjoy these weekend excursions, but I also didn't have a choice in the matter. I enjoyed riding in the boat, water skiing and tubing. I did not enjoy roughing it in a tent and being surrounded by adults who liked to partake in libations of alcohol. I associated their giddiness with ignorance. I thoroughly loved my time on the water, but could not wait to get back home to my snug bed and the quietness of my room.

Event #1: On the last day of my freshmen year in high school, I was getting ready for school when I heard a gunshot outside the bathroom window. I looked outside, but could not see anything. My mom heard it, went to investigate, and learned our neighbor had taken his own life by shooting himself. He was still alive, and my mom was the first one to the scene. She said she would never forget the gurgling sounds coming from his body. Undeniably, this moment changed my mom forever. I sensed something more and immediately went to the phone to call his estranged wife, but there was no answer.

We quickly learned what had transpired. He had been upset that she had filed for a divorce, went over to where she was living, and shot her in the face when she answered the door. Their young son was still asleep when this happened. I am assuming that her neighbors must have heard the gunshot and called the police. He obviously had come home and then turned the gun on himself.

We did not attend his funeral, but we went to hers, and it was very sad. Their little boy was walked down the aisle by adults on both sides of him, holding his hand as they went up to view his mother's casket. He was looking from side to side not really understanding the full capacity of what was going on. He went to live with his grandparents after that, and I never saw him again. I can only imagine how his life was completely altered in that one instant. His mother and my mom had been best friends, and my mom had just started a new job working with her; Mom felt emotionally unable to return to work, so she quit her job.

Event #2: Our neighbor's brother and his wife moved into the empty house. My mom was friendly to both of them, but was also very upset whenever she saw them because of what she had heard and witnessed at their home.

∞

Shortly after these two events, my mom and stepdad made the choice to leave the area and move to a rural location, so they began the house hunt and found acreage with an old farmhouse near Grand Lake. They used the excuse that we would now live by a lake.

We moved to Big Cabin, Oklahoma in November 1986. The square footage of the "new" old place was substantially less than the home we had been living in. Plus, we only had one bathroom. As a sophomore in high school, I instantly realized I had a huge adjustment ahead of me. This move was literally a culture shock for me. In one swift moment, I went from a class of two hundred students down to just twenty; from living in the suburbs to a very rural area. The advanced classes I had been taking were not offered at my new school, so the school adjusted accordingly - even offering some private instruction and a correspondence class through a college. Thanks to my family, the school district obtained five new students in one day and not wanting us to transfer to another school, they accommodated us however they could.

Mind you, I was definitely thinking my parents should have done a little bit of checking before they just enrolled us in this school. They were pleased with the sign on the highway indicating "Excellence in Education" and impressed there was a satellite on the roof of the school. Both were simply illusions, in my opinion, but who was I to say this, I was a teenager at the time. Fortunately for me, I was able to skip my junior year of high school and graduate a year early.

I did not find my new school or classes to be challenging, and I was bored out of my mind. However, I will say that I learned to type and enriched my love of numbers while there because they did offer an accounting class. I also learned how to cross-stitch. Yes, that's right—cross stitch! In order to make the day go by faster, I was allowed to do crafts in class after I finished my schoolwork. I still have the Christmas ornaments I stitched!

Upon graduation, I enrolled in the nearby junior college and obtained an Associate's degree in Accounting. I will also offer you a sneak peek into the next chapter; I met my future husband at Big Cabin.

∞

REVELATION

As you probably can guess, I have reflected on these experiences extensively throughout the years. What if our neighbor had chosen not to take his wife's life and then his own? What if my mom hadn't found him? What if it didn't bother my mom to see his relatives living in that house? What if we had stayed living in Bixby until I graduated from high school? Of course, I will never know the answers to any one of these specific questions because the events unfolded as they did. I can say for certain that had they not occurred exactly as they did, I would not have met my husband and created our two beautiful, amazing children. I was not included in the decision making process; yet the choices that were made, affected my life and my path tremendously.

MESSAGE FOR YOUR JOURNEY

Observe the blessings within your life and give thanks for all of your experiences even if they are different than what you had originally planned. When circumstances occur beyond your control, and they appear to be or feel less than desirable, choose to make lemonade with the lemons. In other words, choose to experience the sweetness rather than the sourness of the situation. Look for the positive. Each experience lends itself to having another experience. Each day is a new beginning and an opportunity to have numerous experiences for personal growth and learning.

TOOL FOR YOUR JOURNEY

Write down your thoughts, feelings, and emotions as you spend time in reflection. Pay attention to bodily sensations as well. Read back through and reflect on what you have written as you are guided to do so. Connect the dots from your lemon experience(s) to where you are today to help you see how situations, that we might not love at the time, actually help us on our journey.

• 6 •
Starting my Own Family

LESSON LEARNED

When you look at your life, the greatest happinesses are family happinesses. ~ Joyce Brothers

I am an amazing wife and mother.

∞

MY STORY

AS I PREVIOUSLY MENTIONED, ONE of the positive things that came out of moving to Big Cabin was meeting my husband, Brooks. He was in the grade above me, and I actually became friends with his older sister first. She made it very clear to me that he had eyes for someone else and would not be interested in me. I was assigned the locker below his, so we had plenty of moments to meet. Brooks tells this story with a twinkle in his eye on numerous occasions to our kids, saying: "Your mom dropped her books, and I picked them up for her." I will laugh because the real story is that my locker was below his and he wasn't too pleased at first that he had to give up his junk locker, so that I could have one.

A group of us gathered one night after a basketball game, and Brooks and I took that opportunity to get to know one another and have an actual conversation rather than just the usual friendly smile and greeting. We attended the Valentine's Day wedding of mutual friends the next day together and quickly became a couple. We had two memorable dates relatively close to one another. Both dates involved dinner and a concert—Air Supply and Chicago. Most of the time, Brooks would just spend time at my house with me and my family, or I would spend time at his house.

Brooks' parents are artists and would travel to do art shows, and they also had a storefront at Silver Dollar City in Branson, Missouri for many years. On occasion, we would take product to them and enjoy the theme park for a few hours. Just like I had issues with camping, Brooks had issues with visiting the theme park, as it was a symbol of work for him. He was an integral part of the family business and would have to come directly home from school and work for several hours in the evening plus every weekend.

His parents were not only married to one another, but they were also married to their business. Everything they did revolved around their art. Brooks has told me many stories of his childhood and teen years, and most outings included an art show. Art was their livelihood, and as such, the children played an important role in the family business. Brooks and I quickly realized that we were alike in many instances. Our parents influenced our childhood in numerous ways. We made the decision to learn from what we considered to be their parenting mistakes and not make those same choices with our own children.

He asked me to marry him before we even finished high school, and I accepted. An artist himself, Brooks carved a fish to sell to obtain the money to buy me a ring. His parents actually kept the woodcarving and returned it to us later as a gift. Some trials and tribulations occurred after graduation because Brooks chose to leave the family business and begin working for my stepdad. His parents were unhappy with his choice for a period of time.

I began college in August of 1988, and we rented a duplex together in Adair in October of that year. I wasn't eighteen yet, but was ready to get out of my parent's house. We both worked to pay our bills, so that I could attend college. Brooks and I were married as planned on February 11, 1989, nearly two years to the day after we began dating. We moved to Claremore a few months later, so that I could be closer to school, and the following year I graduated in May of 1990. I definitely wanted to continue my education, but the nearest four-year university was several hours away; I had to let that dream go—for the time being. We quickly moved back to Big Cabin and purchased a mobile home to put on my parents' property. We stayed in the mobile home until 1995, when we purchased the house we are currently living in.

Brooks and I made the conscious choice to have a baby, and our son was born in January 1992. Life as we knew it changed. We no longer were responsible for just ourselves. We brought life into this world, and we definitely wanted this baby boy. The ultrasound I had previously offered no indication of the baby's gender, and I was really hoping for a little girl. I even brought my own baby dress to the hospital in hopes of the baby being a girl, and Brooks had to make a trip to the store to locate something to bring our baby boy, Cody, home from the hospital in. Our son can truthfully say, "My parents met, fell in love, got married and desired to create a beautiful family." Three years later, we made the conscious choice to have another baby, and our daughter, Caitlin, was born in May 1996.

The words "I love you" were and are frequently expressed in our household, including the physical expression of these words with hugs and kisses. I cannot ever remember my own dad verbally saying those particular words. He chooses to say "Take care," which, I understand now, is more comfortable for him. My mom has always been loving and affectionate. Brooks and I wanted our children to know that they are loved, so we have always made it very clear – by telling and showing them.

Our children are my world and mean everything to me. I know that I can say the same for Brooks as well. My life for many years revolved around my children and their needs. I have encouraged them both to ask questions, to be open, to share their experiences — as these were things that I wasn't allowed or even encouraged to do. I invited them to dream big and go for the gold — to set goals for themselves and to aim high.

With that said, my husband likes to tell me repeatedly that maybe I influenced them a little too much. Bear in mind that Brooks is a perfectionist with his work and his art. He wants to make sure that it is exactly how he wants it done because both are a reflection of him. Combine his perfectionism with my type-A personality, and the result is two kids who strive to be the best in everything they do. I'm not sure this is an entirely "good" thing. I know that I have encouraged them both to lighten up because I have realized - gleaning from my own experiences - that this trait is not altogether a healthy one. I have allowed them the freedom to express themselves; yet I have been, and will continue to be, readily available to both of them when they need me.

∞

REVELATION

To begin with, I cannot believe how many years have passed since I met my husband. Where has the time gone? I still feel young and can hardly believe how old our children are now. I see both of them making plans and life choices for themselves. I am proud and know that Brooks and I followed through on the parenting goals we set for ourselves. While our son no longer relies on me daily, I still find it comforting when he calls or emails me with a question. Well into his final year of college and working full-time, he is dedicated to completing his engineering degree and has already established many goals for his future. Our daughter is in her final year of high school and is also taking concurrent classes at a nearby junior college. She has set some lofty goals for herself as well. She is blossoming and truly coming into her own, and I am proud to be an example for her.

MESSAGE FOR YOUR JOURNEY

Make sure that you tell your loved ones that you love them and to show them as well. Do not allow any words to remain unspoken. Cherish the memories you create and express your gratitude for that which you are thankful for. Recognize that everyone is having their own human life experience, although our experiences are interwoven within our relationships. As parents, our children look up to us as role models. Embrace this role with strength and gratitude. Allow them the opportunity to be who they are, to express their opinions and emotions, and to walk their own path. Encourage your loved ones to reach for the stars and to live life joyfully without regret. Be proud of them, and most of all, be proud of yourself.

TOOL FOR YOUR JOURNEY

Verbally express to your friends and family what they mean to you using whatever terminology feels right and is comfortable for you. Communicate your feelings openly and honestly without hesitation. Take the time to send a card or handwritten letter through the mail. This demonstration of emotion will have a tremendous effect.

• 7 •
What's Wrong with Me Now?

LESSON LEARNED

Health is a state of complete physical, mental and social well-being, and not merely the absence of disease or infirmity.
~ World Health Organization, 1948

**I recognize that past experiences
can contribute to present health issues.**

∞

MY STORY

WHEN OUR DAUGHTER WAS IN the third grade and our son in middle school, I didn't feel right. It was hard for me to actually convey with words exactly how I was feeling. Nonetheless, I visited my local doctor who proceeded to refer me to a specialist. I was lethargic, had no energy, gaining weight without changing my diet, and my menstrual cycle went haywire for lack of a better term. I had swollen lymph nodes in my groin and armpits, and I just plain felt horrible.

I began seeing an oncologist who was trying to figure out a diagnosis, and even she was perplexed. I had numerous blood tests and several CT scans, plus a few other high dollar tests that I cannot recall the names of. My case was complicated, so she chose to begin with ruling out what I didn't have rather than trying to determine what I did have. I visited a dermatologist to have a biopsy for the raised bumps on my fingers. I visited a surgeon to have a biopsy on the lymph nodes. They opted to remove and biopsy a few nodes in my groin area rather than under the arm pit. Neither biopsy provided a definitive diagnosis.

After numerous oncology office visits with no change in symptoms, another CT scan was ordered with a definite and noticeable result. I had a tumor growing in my thymus gland. The thymus gland is part of both the endocrine system and the lymphatic system. Finally, the doctor was able to offer me some resolution, and I was referred to a cardiovascular surgeon to discuss the options available to me. I could have a biopsy to determine if the tumor was benign, but he did not recommend this at all. He indicated that the tumor, regardless of whether it was malignant or benign, would need to be removed due to the location near my heart, and the fact the tumor was increasing in size.

Typically, the thymus gland is larger as an infant and decreases in size as we become older. For whatever reason, my thymus decided to grow and create health issues for me.

I was alone during the consultation with the surgeon, so he asked his nurse to sit in with me. This was by my own choice because I was a big girl and didn't need my husband or anyone else to accompany me for the surgical consultation. I had gone to all the rest of the appointments by myself. The surgeon went over the details of the thymectomy procedure with me, and I attempted to make light of the situation. Jokingly, I asked if it was possible to have a breast reduction and lift while we were operating on that area. Without cracking a smile, he said that it would not be a good idea to do since we didn't know if the tumor was cancerous. I was thinking a two-for-one operation would have been nice, but realistically knew that it wasn't feasible nor was I really being serious. Humor is one of my coping mechanisms as you have probably noticed by the manner in which I have shared some of my personal stories.

My surgery was scheduled, and I wasn't scared. I was ready to start feeling better and assumed that the removal of the tumor would make everything return to normal. I was especially tired of the whacked out menstrual cycle. Enough was enough. The day arrived and my husband and mom were there with me while both of the kids were at school. The last thing I remember is being on the gurney in the operating room telling those in attendance who I was and why I was there. I also made it emphatically clear that under no circumstances did I want any type of urinary catheter. I had a flashback to the pain I experienced when they utilized one while I was in labor with my son. My bladder was full and inhibiting the delivery, so they opted to use a catheter to empty it—definitely an unpleasant feeling I can still recall.

The surgery went as planned, and I woke up in my private hospital room. I was hurting all over even with the morphine I had been given. Apparently, I didn't fully realize that in order to have access to this area, they split your sternum and pull it apart moving your rib cage in the process. The pain was enormous. I looked down at my bandaged chest and could see three drainage tubes, but I did not have a catheter "down there." That was good, but what was I thinking? I had to move, get up and walk to go to the bathroom. The nurses brought in a portable toilet and put it by the bed so I just had to sit up and scoot over rather than walk. Still, this was not the best choice I could have made, but I was not caving in at that point for sure.

It wasn't long before I realized that my dad came to be there with me. He didn't tell me or anyone else he was coming; he just showed up and there he was. I became very emotional. My mom thought he was upsetting me. Instead, I was very happy and surprised; the feelings were just not being expressed accordingly because of the state I was in. My dad stayed with me the first night and slept on the couch in my room. It was a rough night with very little sleep for either of us. He decided to let Brooks stay with me the next night, and he stayed with the kids. I'm not sure my dad has any idea how much this gesture meant to me and the impact that it had on our relationship. He was there for me when I needed him the most, and I didn't have to ask him to come.

I came home and the recovery wasn't happening as fast as I thought it would. The pain was more intense in my spine rather than the sternum. I was unable to drive and had to sleep on the couch because I could not get in and out of the bed for several weeks. Our dachshund, Odie, stayed right by my side through it all and even slept on the couch with me. My husband had to cook, clean, and do the laundry—all of the things I normally did for everyone else. The kids pitched in as well. I was normally the caretaker. This time I was the one being cared for.

For quite some time, I was very self-conscious of the six inch downward scar on my chest and the three half-inch drainage tube scars crossways below it. I now embrace these scars fully—well, almost. They are a daily reminder of my experience.

∞

REVELATION

Reflecting on this health issue, I recognize that I energetically manifested this tumor in my thymus gland. Located in the Heart Chakra, the issue occurred in this particular area because of the frustration and pain that I felt as a child, especially towards my dad. This energetic and emotional pain evolved into a tangible form that needed to be removed, and I recognize that my dad's appearance at the hospital greatly assisted in my healing as well. It was necessary for me to have this experience, so that I could fully understand and help people with their own healing.

MESSAGE FOR YOUR JOURNEY

Assess the health issues you may be experiencing in your own life. Is there a root cause that you can identify due to the location and nature of the issue? Allow yourself to recognize what you are feeling as well as to release and/or resolve any underlying emotions you have neglected to formerly acknowledge. Honor yourself and your emotions as you process what you are feeling. A little bit of self-evaluation now may save a trip to the doctor down the road.

TOOL FOR YOUR JOURNEY

Take a moment to write down your health concerns so that they may be addressed accordingly. If you are guided, I recommend referencing Louise L. Hay's book, Heal Your Body. This book offers mental causes for physical illness and the metaphysical way to overcome them. I personally refer to this book whenever a health issue arises so that I can immediately acknowledge its manifestation and investigate what the underlying causes for the illness might be. Remember to practice discernment and acknowledge what feels right to you.

• 8 •
I Stopped Existing and Started Living

LESSON LEARNED

We are always getting ready to live, but never living.
~ Ralph Waldo Emerson

I am living my life to the fullest degree possible.

∞

MY STORY

One of the most tragic things I know about human nature is that all of us tend to put off living. We are all dreaming of some magical rose garden over the horizon - instead of enjoying the roses that are blooming outside our windows today.
~ Dale Carnegie

HEARING THE STATEMENT AT SOME point along the way, "Your life is what you make of it," made me really question if I was truly living my life to the fullest degree possible. You mean it is not already planned out for me in its entirety? I can actually alter the course of my existence by the choices that I make?

When I was younger, I knew that I wanted to go to college, get married, and have two children as well as the "proverbial house with the white-picket fence." Well, along the way, life happens and our vision becomes slightly altered, and we make choices: we adjust and make lemonade or we do not.

At this point in my life, I somehow got caught up in the motions of a routine and began feeling less than fulfilled. Each day was the same—I would wake up in the morning, go to work, take care of my family duties, go to sleep, and then would start over the next day with the same routine. My vitality for life was nonexistent. Drudgery is a harsh term, but living life was feeling like a chore.

As a wife and mother, I tended to put everyone else before me. I was literally that pot on the back burner of the stove - the pot you stir occasionally, but are not too worried about because you've kept the heat turned low. Well, sometimes we altogether forget about that pot, and its contents become scorched. It didn't take long for me to quickly realize that all the pots on the stove are equally important and should be stirred accordingly.

∞

It is only when we silent the blaring sounds of our daily existence that we can finally hear the whispers of truth that life reveals to us, as it stands knocking on the doorsteps of our hearts.
~ K.T. Jong

This realization began gradually over many years and amplified when I saw Randy Pausch appear on *The Oprah Winfrey Show* in October 2007. He was asked to deliver a reenactment of his original lecture, which he presented on September 18, 2007 as a professor of computer science at Carnegie Mellon University in Pittsburgh, Pennsylvania as part of the university's last lecture series. His book, *The Last Lecture*, was released in April 2008 and provides a written summary of his actual lecture. The lecture's topic, Really Achieving Your Childhood Dreams, was intended to provide personal insight concerning his life lessons as well as give advice to students on how to achieve their own career and personal goals. In reality, it was Randy's last lecture since he was actively dying from pancreatic cancer. The lecture he gave had a dual purpose: (1) He wanted to provide a lasting legacy for his three children, and chose to speak about the importance of overcoming obstacles, of enabling the dreams of others, and of seizing each and every moment or opportunity; and (2) He also wanted to inspire and empower those in attendance that day.

Randy's positive outlook on life continued until his death. He asserted, "I'm living like I'm dying. But at the same time, I'm very much living like I'm still living." His final remarks revealed the following wise words, "It's not about how to achieve your dreams. It's about how to lead your life. If you lead your life the right way, the karma will take care of itself. The dreams will come to you."

Randy lost his battle to pancreatic cancer on July 25, 2008 at the age of 47, but his words will continue to inspire me and the individuals who choose to read his book or view his video. Reflecting on the moment I initially watched the re-creation of the lecture on Oprah, I remember feeling overwhelmed with emotion. Randy appeared to be in excellent health as affirmed by a demonstration in which he began doing push-ups on the stage. In reality, he was a man facing death. His positive attitude about living while dying was extraordinary and touched me deeply.

Throughout his lecture and ensuing book, Randy never

mentioned any regrets or things he wished he had done differently in his life. Many people, including myself, would probably have never heard of Randy Pausch had it not been for the topic of his lecture and the fact that it was literally his last.

Immersing myself in Randy's book and with his accomplishments as my example, I reached inward and found the courage to allow myself to live. I took time to assess what I wanted to change in my life; then went about creating this change. I quickly realized the importance of taking care of me, loving me for who I am and the impact this has on my well-being. Rather than observing life and what was happening around me, I began to actively participate instead of just sitting on the sidelines. I began to speak my truth versus keeping my mouth shut and holding on to those unspoken words and feelings. I consciously and actively chose to stop existing and to start living my life.

I felt like a beautiful butterfly emerging from a long dormant cocoon. I was on the cusp of something new and exciting, and I could feel the power of what was to come... my journey into consciousness.

∞

REVELATION

Making the decision to stop existing and to start living transformed my life in a multitude of ways. My perception of life and all of my life experiences shifted. I recognized that from the moment we breathe the breath of life, we are beginning to die. There is no guarantee that we will live for any length of time. Therefore, it is essential to live each day as though it may be our last. In doing so, no words will be left unspoken and no wishes will remain unfulfilled. I tell my family and friends that I love them whenever I speak to them. I do not hesitate to do something if it is something that I really want to do. In other words, I have learned not to worry if I can afford to do it; I trust that it will work out. My husband is both supportive and encouraging of my spiritual studies, and I have had the opportunity to study with several spiritual teachers in the past few years. Simply speaking, there are people who talk about doing things and then there are people who do the things they talk about. I have gone from being the caterpillar to the butterfly.

MESSAGE FOR YOUR JOURNEY

I encourage you to begin living your life fully right now if you are not doing so already. Do not wait until it is too late to do or say something that you want to do. As the adage goes, "Take time to stop and smell the roses." I encourage you to take time from your busy schedule and listen to the advice Randy has to offer. Watching Randy's lecture and reading his book, *The Last Lecture*, has had a tremendous impact on my own life, and I know it will assist others on their journey, too.

Choosing change and then identifying the change you desire within your life is the first step. It is equally necessary to begin taking time for you on a regular basis. Cultivating the relationship you have with yourself will nourish your soul resulting in a ripple effect in the relationships you have with others.

TOOL FOR YOUR JOURNEY
Choosing Change

It is imperative that you acknowledge, recognize, and identify exactly what aspects of your life you desire to change. Be honest with yourself. Do not allow another individual to influence what you choose to change. This is your life! It is no one else's, and so it is up to you to decide what you want for your life: You make the choice to simply exist or to live your life to the fullest degree possible.

I invite you to do a mini life review about how you're living your life and how you want to live your life. Look deep inside and assess how you feel as you write down the thoughts that come into your immediate awareness. At some point, I recommend that you spend some time reflecting on the changes you wish to make, as well as what you desire to achieve and manifest. Take time to write these thoughts on paper. A thought becomes tangible once it is written on paper. It takes form. You can see the words and touch the paper. Read through what you have written. Read it again aloud and really listen to what you are saying. Review and assess how you feel when reading the words you have written on the paper. Your physical, mental, and emotional responses to these questions are a good indicator of the change you desire. Allow yourself to be present and process what you are feeling. Recognize the impact these words have on your being. Breathe in deeply and exhale as you begin to move forward.

INTERMISSION

Just when the caterpillar thought the world was over,
it became a butterfly. ~ Proverb

RATHER THAN IMMEDIATELY WRITING ABOUT my spiritual awakening, I have opted to include this intermission as a way of acknowledging that the experience was a gradual one instead of instantaneous. As with all celebratory events, I have designated a specific date to remember and honor. I found my voice in 1999 and began speaking my truth. I recognized later that I had an opportunity to wake up at that time as well, but missed it. I began visiting psychics in search of answers. In reality, the answers I had been seeking were within me all along. I now believe that the time wasn't exactly right, and I would not have been ready for this realization.

I had my first psychic reading in the summer of 1999 in Eureka Springs, Arkansas. Venturing into the White Light new age store, I was both curious and fascinated by the reader and his surroundings. I remember the smell of incense and the familiarity of what I was experiencing with all of my senses. Listening intently to what he told me, I knew that this was just the beginning.

Embarking on this spiritual journey, I quickly realized that I am not alone. Even though I had no one to talk to about my experiences, I did not feel alone on my journey. For much of my life, I knew things, but wasn't sure how I knew what I knew. I realize this sounds confusing because it was equally confusing for me. At times, this knowledge would literally freak me out. I was raised in the Baptist religion, which was extremely fear-based from my perception.

I never felt like I had to go to church to connect with God because God was within me. I knew that he definitely was not a man in the sky. I believed that hell wasn't below us and that heaven was all around us, and I felt that the destination hell, for all general purposes, did not even exist - people could be living in hell while on Earth.

I distinctly remember analyzing as a child how I could be alive: "I am breathing. My heart is beating and blood is flowing through my veins. How is all of this even possible?" When the television miniseries, *Out on a Limb*, aired in 1986, I watched it and was enthralled with Shirley MacLaine's autobiographical story. I could feel a switch flip in my brain with an innate understanding of what was to come. Thus began my spiritual journey; even though I was not yet fully awake and spiritually conscious.

During my journey, I have learned and acknowledged that heaven is actually the Spirit realm, also known as the Afterlife. Our loved ones who have passed are there waiting for us to make the transition although they are not actually waiting. They are "living" their lives – learning, creating, and enjoying what makes them happy. I believe that the Afterlife is lush and beautiful with vivid colors beyond our imagination. The Afterlife is not something to be feared, but rather embraced. It is all around us, just in a different dimension vibrating at a higher level than the third-dimensional earth plane. Our souls stay there until we choose to incarnate again. These discoveries have freed me from the tyranny of worrying about going to hell, and given me courage to forge ahead on my path of learning and discovery.

• SECTION TWO •

Spiritual Awakening and Self-Discovery

This section begins with my spiritual awakening, which I officially designate as May 1, 2008.

I began journaling my spiritual path at that time and have incorporated excerpts from my journals.

My objective in chronicling these personal "aha" moments of learning and clarity is to assist and support my fellow sojourners.

• 9 •
Waking Up with Reiki

The secret art of inviting happiness
The miraculous medicine of all diseases
Just for today, do not anger
Do not worry and be filled with gratitude
Devote yourself to your work. Be kind to people.
Every morning and evening, join your hands in prayer.
Pray these words to your heart
and chant these words with your mouth
Usui Reiki Treatment for the improvement of body and mind
~ Reiki Ideals by Usui Mikao

**By allowing ourselves to heal, we assist
with the healing of others.
Healing is an on-going process.**

I REMEMBER, EVEN AS FAR back as when I was a child, wondering exactly what my purpose is in this life. I asked the questions we all ask — Who am I? Why am I here?

What am I supposed to be doing? Is this all there is? What's next?

A very clear answer to my questions was revealed to me on May 1, 2008 through an angel reading. After spending some time searching the Internet for someone to tell me about my angels and connect me with my loved ones who have passed, I found someone to do just that—Steffany Barton of Angels Insight in Overland Park, Kansas. I patiently waited two months for the phone appointment and recognize the date as a pivotal one in my life.

The reading began as follows:

> *I just have to tell you — you are a healer. Your soul is here to help change the world. You are a healer. You have come here to shine your Light, so that you can remind other people of the truth of who they are... you are here to shine your Light, so that others can remember the truth of who they are. You — allowing yourself to be a channel for Spirit, allowing yourself to smile and to listen and to be available to people when they are in need and to see them differently than they see themselves. That's how you change the world and that's how you heal hearts, one by one by one by one...*

Hearing Steffany speak these words to me, I literally had the cartoon light bulb "Ah-ha" moment. As with many other people, I know now that I was born during this period of time for a purpose. She specifically asked me during the reading if my hands shook and if I had ever felt my hands get hot, and they did. She said that after the reading she wanted to talk to me about Reiki, which I had heard of but never experienced, as she was also a Reiki Master. I had previously experienced a Crown Chakra Light Work session with a healer in Eureka Springs, Arkansas, so I was familiar with energy work.

The angel reading I had with Steffany was comprised of messages from angels and loved ones in Spirit as well as pertinent past life information. It was my first exposure to an actual mediumship reading. My grandfather, father-in-law and the child I lost in a miscarriage came through. The messages were very real and very powerful. I knew at that time that I would also be doing this work. I knew that I did not want to simply offer messages to others; I want the mediumship experience to be healing just as it was for me.

I began my Reiki training with Reiki Master Steffany Barton in September 2008 with Levels I and II. December 2008, I was attuned as a Reiki Level III practitioner and completed Reiki Master training in February 2009. I received this encouraging email message from Steffany shortly after completing my Reiki Master attunement, "Thanks again so much for coming to the class. I just wanted to tell you that you have the clearest, most pure connection to Reiki and Source of anyone I have ever trained. And that's over one hundred people. I know that you will go on to become a very important Reiki teacher, so have confidence using the symbols and opening yourself to receiving new symbols. And, start writing about your journey."

I continued my Reiki studies and in August 2010, I was attuned by Steffany to Karuna Reiki®, which was created by William Lee Rand of the International Center for Reiki Training. With each Reiki attunement, my awareness increased substantially. I kept notes on this particular attunement:

The class was really amazing. The energy and attunements were really amazing. The Karuna Reiki® energy is very powerful, and I can feel it all over instead of primarily in my hands when I do a treatment. We spent Monday afternoon talking and learning and then received the Karuna Reiki® I Master attunement. I left Steffany's house at 4:00 pm, picked up food and checked into the hotel room. I read most of the manual and then went to sleep at 7:30 pm. I woke up early the next morning and saw "someone" sitting in the chair next to me very briefly. I fell back asleep and then woke up again to sound blasting only in my left ear and then saw two more visions. I could not really make out details, but they were both different. I tried to move and was unable to, but opened my eyes and saw a dozen or so orbs of light suspended in the air. Everything happened in less than a minute.

I read the rest of the manual and went back to sleep until the alarm went off at 9:00 am. In class, I received the Karuna Reiki® II Master attunement, and then we worked on each other. There were seven people giving Reiki to one person on the table. We took turns leading and calling symbols and then would discuss what we felt. I went third for leading, and the energy really radiated; it was so nice. I was the last person to be on the table and could feel the heat on my Heart Chakra and Crown Chakra. One of the students told me that she had to stand back because of the light emanating from my body. We practiced giving attunements and then I headed home at 4:00 pm. Steffany did tell me after the first class that she thought I would be a great healer. I told her that this was quite a complement to receive, especially coming from her. I should mention that I was drawn to Steffany's energy immediately and found it extremely necessary to complete all of my Reiki training and attunements with her.

Before proceeding any further and because Reiki is so instrumental and pivotal in my own journey into consciousness, you might like to know a little bit more about Reiki in order to understand what it is and why this practice is so very powerful...

∞

WHAT IS REIKI?

According to information derived from The International Center for Reiki Training's website and training manuals, Reiki is deemed a stress reduction and relaxation technique that promotes healing. The Japanese word Reiki means universal life energy. The Reiki technique is a simple hands-on healing modality that is easy to learn and perform, but one must be attuned to the Reiki energy in order to be considered a Reiki practitioner. Reiki practitioners assist in facilitating harmony and balance in the Universe, and they are a conduit for others who want to balance their own body, mind, and Spirit.

The origin of Reiki can be traced to ancient Tibet thousands of years ago and was reintroduced in Japan during the late 1800's by Dr. Mikao Usui of Japan. More recently, Reiki was first introduced in the United States in 1937 by Mrs. Takata and her teacher Dr. Hayashi, who was a medical doctor.

Simply speaking, we are alive because Life Force is flowing through us. We are made up of energy. Every cell in our body is energy. Reiki energy comes from God, which is Source energy, to the practitioner and through his or her hands to aid in healing. The Reiki practitioner is simply a channel for the healing energy that flows through him or her. Their hands are conduits for energy - balancing energy within and around the body. The energy goes where it is needed most. It moves out blocked energies, cleanses the body of toxins, and works to create a state of balance on all levels: physical, mental, emotional, and spiritual. Health is the free and balanced flow of energy. Disease or illness results when the flow of energy is interrupted.

Reiki heals by flowing through the affected parts of the energy field and charging them with positive energy from God/Source. Reiki clears, straightens, and repairs the energy pathways, allowing energy to flow freely in a healthy pattern. The intent is to realign and strengthen the flow of energy as well as to decrease pain, ease muscle tension, speed healing, improve sleep, and to generally enhance the body's natural ability to heal itself.

As a complementary therapy, Reiki enhances traditional or alternative medical care by speeding the healing process. Recognizing that each individual possesses the ability within themselves to do their own healing, the Reiki practitioner's role is purely one as a facilitator to provide an opportunity for self-healing. Reiki provides a means of restoring energy while one is recuperating. It is calming, relaxing, and balancing and can be used anytime and anywhere. Reiki is not used to diagnose or treat specific illnesses. Rather, Reiki practitioners focus on restoration, rebalancing and harmonizing the energy flow in order to promote relaxation, decrease stress and anxiety, and increase a person's general sense of well-being.

During a Reiki session, the individual is seated or lying down fully clothed. The practitioner's hands are placed along energy centers and pathways on the head, neck, chest, abdomen, legs, and feet. Generally, the hands are not actually touching the body, but remain several inches above in the aura because the energy goes to where it is needed.

Reiki treats the whole person, including body, emotions, mind and Spirit, creating many beneficial effects that include relaxation and feelings of peace, security and well-being. The individual receiving Reiki may experience warmth, coolness, gentle tingling, sleepiness, feeling refreshed or perhaps just deep relaxation during the session. They may even have heightened awareness and/or psychic occurrences, such as clairvoyance or clairaudience.

It should be noted that Reiki has very much become part of the 21st century. Well-known hospitals, such as the Mayo Clinic, Johns Hopkins, MD Anderson Cancer Center, and the Cancer Treatment Center, promote Reiki as a complementary approach to medical treatment on their websites. Several Cancer Treatment Center locations now include Reiki in their innovative Mind-Body Medicine Program.

Dr. Oz, one of the leading cardiovascular surgeons in the United States has publicly supported Reiki through his television program. He has allowed the use of Reiki during open-heart surgeries and heart transplant operations stating, "Reiki has become a sought-after healing art among patients and mainstream medical professionals." His wife is a Reiki Master as well.

We know that Reiki works through the distribution of energy along specific channels in our body, and the scientific community is now looking at the benefits that Reiki delivers to both the practitioner and the client. Scientific studies to determine the benefits of Reiki are under way. Although modern medicine has tended to focus more on the physical aspects of healing, we are coming full circle learning that healing is more holistic when we incorporate these "mind, body, Spirit techniques." Reiki can be used for any health issue or condition, but it is not a replacement for proven conventional care or reason to postpone seeing a doctor about a medical problem. Reiki is a wonderful and effective complementary therapy.

To reiterate, Reiki is a Japanese technique for stress reduction and relaxation that promotes healing. Everyone is made up of energy and can channel Life Force energy. To practice Reiki and be called a Reiki practitioner, one must be attuned to it and learn the technique. Level I, also known as the first degree, focuses on opening up the physical body, so that it can accept and channel greater quantities of the Life Force energy and is the foundation for all the other degrees. It is also a permanent attunement to the Reiki energy. Once attuned, a person may channel Reiki energy for healing oneself and others.

The second degree focuses on opening the emotional

body to the Reiki energy. During this level, the student learns about remote healing and mental/emotional healing and receives symbols to increase the power from the Reiki source. Intuitive abilities are heightened as well.

The third degree is the designation of Reiki Master, a teacher of Reiki. The emphasis of the energy is on the spiritual level. The student is attuned to the full Reiki energy, learning additional symbols to increase the power from the Reiki source.

To learn more about Reiki and its benefits, I encourage you to visit William Lee Rand's website, The International Center for Reiki Training, at reiki.org.

∞

WORKING WITH REIKI

Reiki has transformed my life extensively. I am now calmer, more relaxed and much less a Type-A personality than I used to be. I think my husband and kids can vouch for that! My former obsessive-compulsive tendencies are diminished to the point that they are barely noticeable. I used to be a housecleaning fanatic, but not so much anymore. Yes, my house is cleaned regularly, but I no longer obsess over making sure I do it on a certain day and in a particular way. I actually allow and encourage my husband and kids to assist me (even though they may not be doing it the way I would!)

I used to allow people, especially my family, to get under my skin and irritate me to no end. I had always continually sought approval from those around me only to be disappointed or told something that would inevitably hurt my feelings. This does not happen anymore. If I start to feel stressed, the Reiki "kicks in" and chills me out. This also occurs when I have to wait in a long line to pay at a store. Having patience has obviously been one of my life lessons, and I am finally passing the patience course with the help of Reiki.

I know my husband and kids were a bit apprehensive and skeptical when I first started practicing Reiki. Brooks quickly became a believer after just a few sessions. My analytical son always likes for me to scratch his back and his head. The Reiki would "kick in," and he could feel my hands getting hot. He would say, "Mom, you better not be giving me Reiki." Although I have never actually given him a session, he knows that by just being around me he will probably get a good healthy dose.

I'm smiling now as I am reflecting on my Reiki experiences over the past few years. In the beginning, I didn't ground and protect my energy very well. I would have to rest after a session because I was so tired after taking on my client's "stuff" during the session. It didn't take long for me to learn to effectively do both—ground and protect my energy. I should mention that this is something that everyone should do even if you are not practicing Reiki. Each one of us is having our own human life experience. With that experience, we accumulate "stuff" in our energy field. It is a good idea to protect our own energy field from others' "stuff." *Note: I have provided the tools for grounding, centering and protecting your energy in Section Three of this book.*

In addition, I quickly realized that I am clairsentient, also known as an empath, which means I feel what others are feeling physically and emotionally. While offering Reiki to a client during a session, my right wrist suddenly began hurting. I continued to Reiki her, ignoring my wrist pain. Finally, I listened to the guidance I was receiving and began to Reiki her wrist. In that moment, my own wrist ceased to hurt and an image of two golden angel wings filled my third eye. From that point on, I would acknowledge wherever I felt discomfort on my physical body, Reiki that area for my client and the pain would cease on my physical body. Acknowledge and then release — it is as simple as that for me now.

Reiki can be done in-person or distantly as energy is not limited by time or space.

When doing a distant session, I schedule a time that is convenient for my client to relax undisturbed for the length of the session. At the designated time, I go out to the cabin behind our house where the Reiki table is. This cabin is my sacred space. I will light a candle, play music, and perform the session as if the individual was with me in person. I place the name and/or picture of the individual on a healing crystal along with the distant healing symbol and Reiki it as if these items were the actual person. I keep a notebook and write down any sensations I am feeling on my body. As part of this service, I provide any guidance and messages that I receive during the session as well and email everything to the client when the session is over.

∞

Certain individuals find it hard to fathom how Reiki is even possible. Prior to starting a session with my client, I explain what I will be doing and mention some bodily sensations they may feel. I also invite them to ask questions. I smile and tell them to not try to figure out how it is possible and simply allow it to happen. I encourage them to open their heart to believe in something other than what they know. I have noticed that when they stop trying to analyze what is going on, they are typically amazed. In other words, allow yourself the opportunity to go with the flow and simply trust in the process. After the session, I urge my clients to discuss what and how they felt throughout the session. I note any areas I felt discomfort on my body as well as provide messages that I received.

As a Reiki Master, I have the ability to teach and attune others to the Reiki energy. I am honored to have been selected by my students to be their teacher. I have strived to instill within each one of them the recognition of the powerful being that they are as well as the importance of honoring their Light. Coming from a place of love and compassion, I encourage my students to listen to their intuition when practicing Reiki rather than feeling confined to abiding by a set structure or specific technique as some teachers prefer. First and foremost, I encourage them to simply open their heart to love and be love, and the rest will follow.

∞

WAKING UP

Being attuned to Reiki really assisted me with waking up spiritually and psychically. I began seeing energy and Spirit sometime before then and was even told by my eye doctor that I had floaters; otherwise known as eye debris. Yes, that's right! I went to the eye doctor when I first started seeing things to have my eyes checked. When I am outside in the daylight, I can see ripples and waves like I am looking in water. I see orbs and "squiggles" too. I can see energy moving and what I would describe as DNA strands, grouped octagonal shapes, moving lines and sparkles. When I lay down to sleep at night in the darkness, I see symbols and colors with my eyes shut as well as with them open. This was just the beginning of what was to come.

Reiki opened the door, and I chose to walk through it. Even as I began my journey with Reiki, I knew that there was more to come. I have a desire and willingness to work with Spirit, and I am excited to watch it unfold. Patience was a huge issue at first, as I wanted it all right in that moment—here and now. I wanted to see, hear, feel and know Spirit using all of the psychic abilities available. Realistically, I knew that a process was involved. I would only open up to what I could handle at any given time.

• 10 •
Finishing What I Started

*It takes courage to grow up and become
who you really are.* ~ e.e. Cummings

**Live your life fully without regret.
Choose to finish what you started.
The time will pass anyway.**

IT TOOK ME A LONG time and much consideration
to realize the truth of who I really am. Labels, such as
"nerd" or the nicer way of saying it—"the quiet, shy, smart
kid who likes to read"—often adhere themselves to us
physically, mentally and emotionally. These labels tend to
define us and will limit us if we allow them to. What I
mean is that people may not approach you or may think
you are snobby because of their perception of you and your
behavior.

As the oldest child and only daughter, my dad made it

clear to me that he expected great things from all of his children. Anything less than the esteemed A on our report card was unacceptable. My brothers and I were given the treasured $1 per A as an incentive to do well in school. Plus, I remember the added bonus of taking our report card at the end of each nine week period to get ride tickets at a local amusement park.

When I was younger, I wanted to be a teacher. Even in elementary school, my teachers would encourage me to assist the other students with their work during class and help them to understand the assignments. I excelled in school in all areas. I detested the required gym classes probably because I was usually the last one picked for teams. I had no desire to play school sponsored athletics, such as softball or basketball, nor participate in any athletic activity whatsoever. No thank you, that was not for me. I wasn't overweight or out-of-shape; I just didn't like participating in any kind of game, especially when it involved sweat. Maybe I just didn't like being told what to do or how to do it. I liked being the captain of my one-person team just fine.

As previously mentioned, I was able to skip my junior year of high school after changing schools because of the classes (or lack thereof) they offered. This altered my original plans substantially. I attended Rogers State College, a nearby junior college, out of high school, and graduated Summa Cum Laude in May 1990 with an Associates of Arts in Accounting. I will admit that I chose this degree because of the Accounting class offered at Big Cabin and the teacher who taught it. Plus, I was really good at numbers. I am a whiz with the ten-key calculator, too!

I deeply regretted not continuing further with my secondary education and sensed the extreme disappointment within my father as well. In his eyes, a two-year degree was not good enough — period. I knew that I could return to school at any time and was waiting for the perfect time to do so. You know how that goes; you put it off and put it off and before you know it, several years have passed. After our son was born, I decided that I would take a couple of classes and pursue a teaching degree. I applied to be a substitute at a few schools in the area and was accepted at all three of them. I am very thankful that I did this because I quickly realized that I did not have the patience necessary to be a school teacher. That experience was enough to derail my college plans for quite some time.

Finally, after many years of procrastination, I set a goal for myself and decided that I wanted to finish my education before my son graduated from high school, so I set out to do just that. Much to my delight, the junior college I originally attended received the necessary accreditation to become a university, Rogers State University. In addition, a new program, spearheaded by the Oklahoma State Regents for Higher Education, was now available, and I was the perfect candidate. According to the RSU website, "If you once attended college, but didn't complete your degree, Rogers State University has a new program just for you. The new Adult Degree Completion Program is for past students who earned at least seventy-two college credit hours. At RSU, we understand that you have a full-time job and a family to support. We can work around that. The new program is offered in convenient eight-week "mini-semesters" throughout the year at our campuses in Claremore and Bartlesville. Many classes are offered online. You can start at any time. And you can earn a Bachelor degree in as little as eighteen months. This is not an "earn your degree quickly scheme." This is a highly-regarded academic program at an accredited, well-respected institution. At the end, you will earn a Bachelor of Science (B.S.) in Organizational Leadership, a versatile degree that is in-demand by top employers. The program is offered in a flexible, accelerated format to assist more adults in northeast Oklahoma to earn a four-year degree."

This program definitely appealed to me, so I made application to be enrolled in the Business Studies option and was accepted. I returned to school March 2008 enrolling in one eight-week class after speaking with the Dean. His words are still fresh in my mind, "What are you waiting for?" I enrolled in six credit hours for the summer semester as well. I should mention that although several of the required courses for the degree were offered as mini eight-week classes, there was nothing "mini" about the course load. The intent was the ability to focus on one class the first eight weeks of the semester and then focus on the next one the second eight weeks rather than taking two "regular" courses at the same time.

Although most of the classes I took were online, I also attended classes at night the first semester as well as during the day the last semester. It didn't take long for me to get in "college" mode again. I can also say that I was definitely pushed beyond my comfort zone on numerous occasions. Thankfully, Reiki assisted me tremendously during those times especially with studying, taking tests, and giving presentations. Returning to college, as an adult, offered me opportunities for learning and growth literally and figuratively speaking. For two years, all of my free time was filled with doing homework and studying for tests. Gratefully, my husband pitched in and helped me with cooking, laundry, and cleaning—household chores I normally did.

I really love psychology, but I was going to have to take quite a few additional classes if I wanted to switch my major from business since I already had an Associate's degree in Accounting. Plus, the degree program made more sense. Many of the electives I took were in psychology. During the final semester, one of my psychology professors, noticing that I was in two of her classes, asked me if I was minoring in Psychology. To be honest, I didn't even realize that was a possibility. I checked into it, and I only needed one more class to have the minor. I spoke with the professor for the class I needed and was added to the class a week late. I was obsessing about already missing a week of class. I'm "one of those" students who never missed class for any reason whatsoever. There was one seat left in the class and it happened to be by someone I knew. She was the older sister of one of my son's classmates. I wasn't the oldest person in the class by any means, but I was definitely one of the older ones. This was the case in my other classes as well.

I made it a point to meet with all of my professors in person during their office hours to introduce myself. This is something I would do even when I was taking an online class. From my perspective, a person will remember you if you make the concerted effort to introduce yourself. They will put a face to the name when they see it. I passed this advice on to my son, and he has actually listened and incorporated it as well. Since he is attending a large university, he could get lost in the shuffle, so to speak. Attending class is not a requirement and there is no way that the professor could possibly remember every student enrolled in their courses. However, taking the initiative to schedule a time during office hours for a short introduction will pay off enormously. I am not referring to favors by any means. Rather, the professor will more than likely recognize that you are a serious student.

I graduated in May 2010 exactly one week before my son graduated from high school, and exactly 20 years after receiving my AA degree.

Being a self-proclaimed over-achiever as well as having a Type-A personality, I graduated Summa Cum Laude with a Bachelor's degree in Business and a minor in Social Science-Psychology. I was deemed the Outstanding Graduate for the School of Business & Technology and was inducted into not one, but three honor societies for my efforts—Sigma Beta Delta International Honor Society for Business Management and Administration; Alpha Chi Honor Society for Academic Excellence; and Psi Chi National Honor Society in Psychology.

I ordered the cap, gown, and tassel, and I walked during graduation proudly displaying the honor societies' colored cords. I was not going to let this moment pass me by. My husband, children, mom and dad were in attendance. Rather than simply offering his congratulations, my dad stated, "You finally listened to me and got your degree." I chose not to let his words affect me and undermine the joy I was feeling for my accomplishments. I knew that he was proud of me and these words were his way of congratulating me. However, I will admit that I was longing for something a little more from him in that moment. I understand that he is who he is, and I am who I am. I am my father's daughter, but his words and actions do not define who I really am. As I stated before, I used to seek approval from those around me. Even as an adult, I wanted to make sure both of my parents were proud of me.

By taking action and finishing what I started twenty years earlier, this conscious act of completion became the "missing piece in my puzzle." I no longer had the feeling of regret regarding my college education. Consequently, I was guided to move full-steam ahead with my spiritual studies. I continued my Reiki training to become a Karuna Reiki® Master. I studied mediumship under the direction of world-renowned psychic medium Lisa Williams, celebrated medium and best-selling author James Van Praagh, and the esteemed psychic medium John Holland. The ensuing chapters offer more insight on this training.

I am truly enjoying every moment of my life. I have met many amazing individuals and spiritual companions with whom I have shared meaningful and life-changing connections. Knowing who I am and where I desire to go in my soul's purpose, I look forward to waking up each morning and making a difference in the lives of others. My life is unfolding before my eyes, and I am excited to be on this journey — this journey into consciousness! My heart is filled with joy and love as this journey continues.

• 11 •
Transforming at the
Transformation Conference

*Taking readers beyond the unexplained and exploring the
possibilities of the Universe and Beyond.*
~ Ozark Mountain Publishing

THIS CHAPTER HIGHLIGHTS MANY PIVOTAL
experiences on my journey into consciousness, which
occurred over a five year time span. These "steps along the
way" played an important role in my personal and spiritual
growth. Each year's conference provided lessons in self-
discovery and opportunities for learning and growth. Some
colleagues have verbalized their amazement at the spiritual
"fast track" I appear to be on. In reality, I recognize that I
am exactly where I am supposed to be in each and every
moment. Attending this particular yearly transformation
conference, as well as other conferences, has assisted me
tremendously on my spiritual journey.

∞

2009
LESSON LEARNED

The important thing is not to stop questioning. Curiosity has its own reason for existing. One cannot help but be in awe when he contemplates the mysteries of eternity, of life, of the marvelous structure of reality. ~ Albert Einstein

I'm seeing everyone and everything through the eyes of a child.

Dolores Cannon's Ozark Mountain Publishing Transformation Conference came into my awareness in early 2009. This conference was held on June 12-14, 2009 in Rogers, Arkansas, which is just a short ninety minute drive away from my home. According to Ozark Mountain's website, "Ozark Mountain Publishing publishes only non-fiction metaphysical and spiritual material. Our purpose is to provide readers with accurate, interesting, and educational information that opens the mind to fascinating possibilities. We hope that you will take the journey with us and explore the possibilities of the Universe and Beyond."

The website also states, "The speakers at each of the conferences will be a blend of those drawn from Ozark's own pool of fascinating authors and others who have been invited as a complement to Ozark's authors because they are able to speak about topics that no one else is addressing at this level. Both Transformation Conferences are aimed at those who seek transformation at a deep level for themselves, their relationships with others and for the planet."

I truly had no idea what was in store for me that

weekend. Any pre-conceived notions I may have had were quickly exceeded. I attended the conference by myself, yet did not feel the least bit alone. I attended most of the presentations and had several readings that weekend. I felt like a kid in a metaphysical candy store! This conference was my first true venture into the metaphysical realm. I did not hesitate to introduce myself to several of the authors/speakers, including Sherri Cortland, author of the books, Windows of Opportunity, Raising Our Vibrations for the New Age, and Spiritual Toolbox.

As I mentioned briefly in Chapter 2, singer and actress Helen Reddy was the keynote speaker that year. I just so happened to be traveling to Sydney, Australia in July to meet my friend. Living in Tokyo at the time, my friend was going on a business trip and invited me to join her. I had instinctively hesitated because the flight was expensive, but I knew it would be a trip of a lifetime. I understood that I may not have another opportunity presented to me like this one, and that I should forgo the financial worry and just go for it. My friend had to work, and I was going to have several days to explore the city. After finishing her work in Sydney, we would fly to Cairns where the Great Barrier Reef is located and spend a few days there sightseeing.

Making conversation, I introduced myself to Helen and asked her about Sydney since she now lives there. The next day I bought her book, The Woman I Am, and asked her to sign it for me. Helen spoke that night and talked about her spiritual journey and that she no longer entertains, but does hypnotherapy work. I should mention that she has recently come out of retirement and has scheduled a few limited engagements. Long story short, after she spoke, I stood in line to speak with her again and boldly asked if I could have a hypnotherapy session with her while I was in Sydney. I was guided to just ask the question knowing that I had a 50/50 chance of getting the YES answer I was hoping for. If I didn't ask the question, there wasn't a possibility at all. She looked at me and said, "Yes, here is my number. Contact me when you get there." *Note: The rest of this story was previously revealed in Chapter 2; i.e. how Helen served as a catalyst for my transformation.*

The conference ended Sunday with a group regression with Dolores Cannon. Dolores is well-known for her method of past life regression therapy. During the first portion of the group regression, I saw a stone cottage in a field. I was a mother with long dark hair and was wearing a beige dress. My husband was a peasant farmer. He was a big, burly man with a bulbous nose and a beard and mustache. Inside the cottage on the dirt floor, two little boys were eating bread.

Then, Dolores guided us through a future life progression. I immediately saw that I was an Asian man wearing a blue suit. It was a rural barren area with tall apartment buildings. I had no family, but did have a black dog. The landscape was nothing like I had ever seen. Both of these sessions seemed very surreal as I had not experienced anything like it before.

The conference had just ended, yet I was already looking forward to returning the next year. My journey into consciousness had truly begun, and I was beginning to make conscious connections.

∞

2010
LESSON LEARNED

Courage is the power to let go of the familiar.
~ Raymond Lindquist

Moving forward without fear
can have tremendous results.

I was elated to attend the 2010 Transformation Conference on June 18-20, 2010. That year's conference was held at a new venue that was much larger than the year before. Literally, just a few weeks prior to the conference, I contacted Ozark Mountain Publishing to see if they had a vendor table still available as I decided to offer Reiki and sell my mosaics. At the time, they were completely full. I still had a knowing that I would be a vendor. Precisely the day before, I got the call that they had a cancellation, so my attendee ticket was transferred to a vendor booth. I happily gathered up the items for my table and loaded them in the car smiling the entire time.

Once again, I attended most of the lectures. This time I also offered Reiki sessions in my room. The accessibility due to the distance between the convention center and my room was not favorable, but it didn't matter to me. Since that time, I adapted accordingly and began offering chair Reiki sessions in my booth for a shorter period of time.

I met my friends Beth and Bridgette during this conference. Both of these beautiful Lightworkers are raising individual and global consciousness with their work. Beth reads the Akashic records and assists individuals on their spiritual journey. According to the Linda Howe Center for Akashic Studies website, "The Akashic Records are a universal filing system which record every occurring thought, word, and action: a collection of mystical knowledge stored in the etheric levels. The vibrational records of each individual soul and its journey are contained here, making it a profound spiritual resource for consciousness development and expanded spiritual awareness." I can attest that the guidance I have received through Beth has played an integral role in my own transformation.

Bridgette is an extraordinary healer. Truly, there are no words to describe her work because what she does is beyond words. My first session with her was amazing and was nothing I had experienced before. I could feel my energy moving. Although I didn't exactly know what was going on at the time, I could feel energetic shackles being removed from my ankles.

Dannion Brinkley was the keynote speaker on Friday night. I was enamored with him and listened intently to every word he spoke. I remembered watching the 1995 television movie, *Saved by the Light*. This movie was based on Dannion's book of the same name and detailed his near-death experience when he was struck by lightning in 1975 and declared dead for twenty-eight minutes. The term, near-death experience or NDE, refers to the experience of when a Spirit leaves a person's body and travels towards the Light to cross over to the other side. Before doing so, the Spirit returns to the physical body to resume living. Ultimately, Dannion's three near-death experiences have left him with an extraordinary sense of perception. I chatted with him periodically throughout the weekend and even got three hugs from him! For anyone who hasn't experienced a Dannion hug, I have to say they are the most AMAZING hugs ever. For those of you who have, you know exactly what I am talking about! I bought his book, *Saved by the Light*, and had him sign it for me. The inscription inside reads, "To Shelly, I will always love you. Dannion."

The full impact of these words were revealed to me the next night when I attended another lecture. Lindsay Wagner's presentation incorporated her "Quiet the Mind & Open the Heart" technique and included a meditation. Deciding to open up fully, I opted to lie down on the floor with my palms up open to receiving during the meditation. I began feeling sensations all over my body, especially in the palms of my hand. My hands felt very heavy, and I could feel symbols being "burned" into them. Listening to the wordless music, the fourth song sounded like the music from the Whitney Houston/Dolly Parton song, *I Will Always Love You*. Although there were no words, I could hear the words plainly in my mind. The message in the meditation validated the words Dannion had written in my book the day before. I realize both Dannion and Lindsay were simply messengers. I know the message came from God, the angels and my guides who will always love me.

Later that evening, I chatted for a while with my friend, Sherri Cortland. As a Spiritual Growth Accelerator and Secretary to Spirit, Sherri is the author of the books, *Windows of Opportunity*, *Raising Our Vibrations for the New Age*, and *Spiritual Toolbox*. Sherri and I took this opportunity to catch up in person. It had been a year since we had last seen each other. Sherri's first book, *Windows of Opportunity*, was printed immediately after the last conference, and she was invited to return. As a speaker, she also had a booth to sell her beautiful handmade jewelry. Both of us needed to man our booths and greet the conference attendees rather than just sitting there talking to one another all weekend, so we took time this evening to do just that. I felt energized and wide awake, but decided I should go to sleep.

Tossing and turning, I looked at the clock, and it was 1:30 am. Apparently I fell asleep because I woke up, looked at the clock and watched it change from 4:44 to 4:45 *(*Note: As previously mentioned, my birth certificate states that I was born at 4:44 pm)*. I closed my eyes and saw an open book with funny looking words, possibly Hebrew or Sanskrit. I woke up again and heard myself speaking out loud, "Seal the room, and let nothing but the white light in." A flash of white light appeared from my left into my sight. A small sepia colored square was playing like a movie in front of me. This movie showed a man in a motorized wheelchair and several people walking around in an area that looked like the hallway of the convention center. A large man was in front of them holding a microphone or something similar in his hands in front of him. I was observing this scenario from above looking down at an angle. I opened my eyes, and they felt heavy. The clock said 5:35.

I immediately sought out Beth and Bridgette at breakfast and eagerly told them about my experience. I was curious to know if they could detect the shift in me as well and scheduled appointments with them both. Beth was able to accommodate me immediately; the information she provided me during the reading was significantly different than the day before. I had another session with Bridgette at the end of the day. Once again, I could feel waves of energy being lifted from my body during the healing session. Connecting with Beth and Bridgette was very comfortable and seems to have been destined. Having a session with both of them is something that I continue to look forward to each upcoming conference.

Driving home Sunday night, I did not feel like myself at all. I am not even quite sure how I made it home. I felt like I was literally on autopilot. I was energetically wide open that weekend and had two Akashic readings as well as two healing sessions. I woke up Monday morning to a swollen face and didn't even recognize myself. My left eye was almost swollen shut, my mouth looked terrible, and my nose was flattened. I felt horrible! I spent two hours in the bathtub soaking and was hot all day long. I broke out in hives, too. I ended up going to the doctor to get a cortisone shot. The look on the doctor and nurse's faces when I told them that I had been at a transformation conference and had a lot of energy work done was priceless. I now know what a "psychic attack" feels like. I trust that I will be better prepared for next year's conference because I do not want to ever experience this again.

∞

2011
LESSON LEARNED

Do not believe in anything simply because you have heard it. Do not believe in anything simply because it is spoken and rumored by many. Do not believe in anything simply because it is found written in your religious books. Do not believe in anything merely on the authority of your teachers and elders. Do not believe in traditions because they have been handed down for many generations. But after observation and analysis, when you find that anything agrees with reason and is conducive to the good and benefit of one and all, then accept it and live up to it.
~ Buddha

Be discerning and establish boundaries —
both are necessary.

The conference arrived June 10-12, 2011 in Rogers, Arkansas at the same venue it was held at before. That year I sent my vendor application in early. I would be offering readings, chair Reiki in my booth (I learned from last year), and have Reiki-related items for sale, such as chakra candles, crystals and crystal jewelry. Since I was busy working, I attended only a handful of the lectures. Sherri Cortland's presentation was one of them. Her book, *Raising Our Vibrations for the New Age*, was just published, and she would be speaking about that subject. She had asked me to read the rough draft before submitting the final copy of her manuscript to Ozark Mountain Publishing and let her know my thoughts. It was an honor for me to do so, and I happily agreed. In this book, Sherri's Guide Groups concentrated on providing us with tools to use to help us (1) expedite our spiritual growth and complete our "To Do" list for this incarnation with less drama and pain; and (2) increase our vibrational level and positive energy output to make the completion of the Shift easier for everyone and for our planet. Both of Sherri's books are easy to read and understand, and I have included them on my recommended reads list at the end of this book. *Note: Sherri channels the information from her Guide Groups through automatic writing.*

The term, automatic writing, describes writing that is produced while in communication with Spirit. The means of writing may involve using a pen and paper or the keyboard of a computer. A prayer of protection should be invoked prior to communication, and you should always be aware of the entity with whom you are writing.

Fortunately, as a vendor, we receive a DVD copy of the entire conference to watch later, so I wasn't worried about missing out on something. I could revisit the conference while lying on the couch at home and have since done so. I thoroughly enjoyed spending time with my friends Sherri, Beth, and Bridgette as well as making new friends.

My reading with Beth provided me further insight and indicated that I was beginning a seven-year cycle. This knowledge was comforting to me as I could feel a shift from the year before and so could she. On Sunday, I had a healing session with Bridgette.

The unplanned highlight (I'm being sarcastic here) of that year's conference involved a chain of events. These events offered me two spiritual lessons—discernment and boundaries. And I really learned them this year! Discernment is the ability to perceive the messages your Higher Self and body are telling you. For example, if someone tells you something, but it does not feel right, then you can practice discernment and not accept it as your truth. Just because it is their truth does not mean it is your truth.

The boundaries lesson was a little more involved. I

learned that saying no is okay and necessary. If I do not want someone to put their hands on me, specifically regarding an energy healing session, I could tell them, "No thanks. That's not okay with me for you to do so. I have a right to decide who I allow to do this. It is not for you to decide for me."

Also, if I didn't want someone to sit behind my table and visit, I could tell them no. It was my space, and I could decide who I allowed to be in it at any given time. I knew from last year's experience that I did not want to be sick again, so I checked in with Bridgette and made sure that my energetic body was clear and good to go before parting ways with her. I also knew that I should stay the night Sunday night and drive back home on Monday morning.

∞

2012
LESSON LEARNED

The power of accurate observation is commonly called cynicism by those who have not got it. ~ George Bernard Shaw

Observations are good; allowances are better.
Everyone is having their own experience.

The transformation conference was held in Rogers, Arkansas on July 13-15, 2012 at the same location it was the previous two years. Once again, I offered readings, chair Reiki, and had items for sale. I spent time with my friends Sherri, Beth, and Bridgette. A year had passed since I had seen them. Sherri asked me to be her guest at the author's dinner on Thursday night. This was an opportunity for me to listen and learn as well as to meet several of Ozark

Mountain Publishing's authors.

The conference opened on Friday morning, and it felt very different. Perhaps, it was simply that my perception of the experience was radically different from what it was before. I am not sure. Spiritually speaking, I know that I have "grown" a lot over the past year. I observed and absorbed; taking in everything and everyone around me. My boundaries were intact and my awareness was heightened on all accounts. I learned my lessons well. As I am writing this now, the song lyrics, "…it is all right now, I learned my lesson well. See you can't please everyone, so you got to please yourself," just came into my awareness. There was definitely no need for me to have another learning experience on that same subject.

I was looking forward to my yearly healing session with Bridgette and scheduled time with her on Friday evening for "the usual." This year she made extensive notes in comparison to the previous years' sessions.

She noted:

> *You had resentment on yourself for the way life could advance but doesn't. Biting your tongue holds you back from where you are headed, the journey needs to be shortened. Your feet have wings and life's advancement will move quickly from this point on. Hold on for the ride, but keep your eyes peeled for those that wish to distract or derail you. Tests await you. Follow your gut! Your spine is your meter to stress. Stretch and relax and be aware of the signals. You don't need roadblocks on your energy highway. You are birthing plant based nature energy.*

I attended three lectures on Saturday and one of them was Sherri Cortland's. She spoke about living in the present rather than waiting to transition to 5D Earth or the end of the world. At the time of this conference, many individuals were caught up in fear thinking that the world would end on December 21, 2012. They had subsequently put their lives on hold waiting for what may happen. In reality, Mother Earth and her inhabitants have been shifting already. There is not a specific date for the Shift to occur. We are always shifting and growing. It is time to be present and live our lives fully rather than waiting for something to happen.

My reading with Beth on Sunday confirmed and validated what I had already been feeling for myself. I actually listened to the CD recording of last year's reading on my drive over to Arkansas. Every time I listen, I hear something new or will have clarity on something in particular. Much of what she said has happened and is still happening at this time. Beth's readings tap into the Akashic records, yet the manner in which she conveys the information is truly the key. She is a channel in which we connect to ourselves. Through her words and eyes, we see beyond what we know for ourselves at the present time. Her messages are both healing and empowering, which is why I feel so connected to her.

∞

2013
LESSON LEARNED

Everything becomes a little different as soon as it is spoken out loud. ~ Hermann Hesse

Speaking my truth
and honoring my emotions is essential.

Once more, I was excited to attend the conference, which was held at a new venue in Springdale, Arkansas on

July 19-21, 2013. I was a vendor for Ozark Mountain Publishing's UFO Conference held April 12-14, 2013 in Eureka Springs, Arkansas. My table was next to Ozark's book table, and I had the opportunity to chat with "the girls" throughout the weekend. I asked for my table to be next to theirs for this one as well.

This year, I planned a group reading event at the Unity of Fayetteville for Thursday night prior to the conference. I always enjoy these events, and it was the perfect way to start the conference.

The conference began Friday morning and I was happy to re-connect with "old" friends and make new ones. The Shelly Wilson Show (formerly titled Believe in Believing) has been on the air for two years, and I had many authors approach me inquiring about being a guest on the show. I was delighted to meet Garnet Schulhauser in person after communicating via email to schedule him on the show, and here's a little about him:

> *Previously practicing corporate law, Garnet's life changed dramatically one day in 2007 when he was confronted on the street by what he thought was a homeless man named Albert. Over the next few years, he had a series of conversations with Albert, a wise spirit guide in disguise, who disclosed startling new truths about life, death, the afterlife, and God. The first of many books to come, Garnet wrote Dancing on a Stamp at Albert's request, so that these revelations would be available to everyone.*

Sherri Cortland spoke on Saturday afternoon. Unfortunately, issues at the printers delayed her third book, Spiritual Toolbox, so it was not available at the conference. Her presentation focused on the book itself, and how it offers insight, meditations and exercises from twelve souls (six on the other side of the veil and six on this side) to assist Lightworkers in opening up to their missions and facilitating direct communication with Spirit. I am honored to be a contributor to this great reference tool, and three of my meditation exercises are included in the book. As a Lightworker and Spiritual Teacher, I believe that Spiritual Toolbox is an essential read for all who are on a spiritual journey. This is truly a guidebook for Lightworkers, and covers a plethora of topics ranging from the Akashic records to Walk-ins.

In addition to having my yearly reading with Beth and a healing session with Bridgette, I also had the opportunity to experience the Tower of Light Experience (TOL) from conference participant Patrick Moulin along with two of my colleagues. According to Patrick, "The main aspect in the TOL process is to simply allow it. It is this surrendering to one's own heart that guides it. In its own right, to dive into this allowing process is already very precious, because it allows us to open up to and connect with subtler layers or fields that are in and around us." Here is the summation of my experience:

> *I was immediately thankful when Dr. Summer's introduced me to Patrick and Marisa. After chatting with them, I was excited to experience the Tower of Light for myself. Due to time constraints, I asked that they let me know when 20 minutes had passed prior to beginning. Throughout the session, I felt very much at peace. I could feel the energy moving throughout my body with my body swaying gently. I kept seeing lots of colors and enjoyed the sensations I was experiencing. In what seemed like a matter of moments, Marisa gently tapped my shoulder to let me know that 20 minutes had passed. I felt vibrant and re-energized after the session.*

As I write this book, the 2013 transformation conference has just concluded and provided me, once again, with experiences for learning and growth. For the last five years, this conference has continually fed my mind, body and spirit; it has provided the opportunity to bask in the energy of like-minded souls, which is fulfilling on all levels — physically, mentally, emotionally and spiritually.

There wasn't one single experience during the 2013 conference that stands out specifically. Rather, the entire weekend was a beautiful experience. Sharing conversations and meals, reconnecting with individuals I've met before, and making new friends really fed my soul. There were numerous synchronistic events and déjà vu moments — too many to count to be honest.

A lot of clearing occurred during the weekend as well. I found that I was quite emotional on Sunday, but honored myself and what I was feeling. Rather than trying to maintain composure and my emotions, I let the tears flow. I expressed what I was feeling and spoke my truth rather than keeping it inside.

The past five conferences have offered me a wealth of knowledge and also the opportunity to make conscious connections with other individuals who are also on this spiritual journey. I am already looking forward to the next one.

• 12 •
Fellow Travelers on this Journey

Let us be grateful to people who make us happy, they are the charming gardeners who make our souls blossom.
~ Marcel Proust

We are not alone on this journey.

EVERY HUMAN BEING DESIRES TO not only feel loved, but to give love as well. It is innate within each one of us to want to connect with others, to want to be open and to live an authentic life. We want to love and to be loved in return. Expressing love and sharing kindness takes such a small effort, yet has an enormous effect. This ripple of love surpasses anything anyone could imagine if they would simply allow this love to come in. I've learned that anything is possible with love — as love is all there really is. There is an essential need for people to grow together, support one another, and walk together as both human companions and soul companions.

My journey into consciousness has availed me the opportunity to make conscious connections with numerous like-minded souls. Synchronicity, otherwise known as a meaningful coincidence, often time plays a role in the people that cross my path. Since finding my voice, I am not afraid to extend my hand to others and to be the one to speak first. Many wonderful friendships have been formed in this manner.

Recognizing your connection to those people who are in your life today will assist you in understanding the important roles we play in each other's lives. Please remember though to not compare your journey to anyone else's journey as we are all having our own unique human life experiences.

Let me take this opportunity to tell you about some of my fellow travelers and how we met:

Sherri

As I previously mentioned, I first met my dear friend, Sherri Cortland, at the 2009 Transformation Conference. She was one of the speakers and has been a speaker each year since that time. After her presentation, I went to her table to greet her and let her know how much I enjoyed her talk. Sherri's first book, Windows of Opportunity, was not yet available in print, and she was actually there because another speaker cancelled at the last minute. I have no doubt that the Universe played a role here. As soon as Sherri's book was available, I purchased it, read it, and then sent her an email. As I've mentioned before, Sherri is a Spiritual Growth Expeditor, and she channels her Guide Groups through automatic writing. *Windows of Opportunity* was primarily written to help us become consciously aware of, and begin to recognize, the windows of opportunity and relationship villains we personally built into our life plans. Sherri's Guide Group writes that by recognizing these windows of opportunity and taking action to learn the lesson, we will learn our lessons and repay our Karmic debt fast and with less drama and pain.

I can tell you that I learned a lot about many of the relationships in my life as well as several experiences I have had from reading Sherri's book. This was the beginning of a meaningful and balanced relationship. I say this because, looking back, so many relationships I have had with others were, what I now perceive to be, unbalanced and emotionally draining. I can also quite happily say that I have become quite adept at spotting the windows of opportunity and relationship villains in my life. Without a doubt, every experience with another person opens a window for learning and growth.

Sherri and I began chatting on the phone periodically and continued to correspond via email. We looked forward to connecting again in 2010 at the transformation conference and each year thereafter. Sherri's book, *Raising Our Vibrations for the New Age*, was the focus of her presentation in 2011. The book's description on Amazon.com indicates, "A group of entities on the other side of the veil came together for the specific purpose of dictating this material to Sherri through automatic writing."

As they stated, "The purpose of this book is simple. It is to help people make it through the Shift with as little stress and drama as is humanly possible during a sensation of this type, and it is sensational as it is something that beings are gathering from all corners of the universe to see. It is something that entities would give their 'soul teeth' to be part of because it is so juicy and so new and so historic. Being on your side and having to worry about weather changes and storms and disasters isn't fun, and we all know that, but on this side we know that every one of you who is there signed up for it and you were chosen to be there. It is not something that you are part of because of bad luck."

She has since published her third book, *Spiritual Toolbox*, and I am delighted to be a contributor to its contents. I feel that, once again, Sherri's new book will assist many of us who have chosen to walk this spiritual path.

Each of Sherri's books has played a pivotal role in my journey into consciousness. Her manner of writing is conversational and easy to understand, much like my own. I always tell her that I can hear her telling me the information as I am reading it. Our friendship is very comfortable with no stress or drama. We put our business minds together quite often and assist one another whenever we can. As a matter of fact, she was the first person to read this book.

∞

Anthony

I met several individuals while attending Lisa Williams Intensive Mediumship Training. Several of us made the decision to apply and were chosen to take her Advanced Mediumship and Platform classes as well. I will write more about those experiences in an upcoming chapter. My dear friend Anthony and I met that life-changing weekend. We were grouped together with several others for a group exercise. I remember looking across the circle at him and him looking back at me. We just smiled with an unspoken knowingness. From my perspective, much was conveyed without words. I believe we sensed a knowingness between us, but were unsure of our connection. Returning home, we connected on Facebook and then subsequently chatted on the phone. Since that time, we have formed a comfortable connection. We recognize and understand that we are in each other's lives for a reason. Inevitably during our chats, we begin to reflect and ponder, taking the conversation to a much deeper level than originally intended. We never plan for these conversations to go this way, but they always do.

∞

Jackie and Robin

During that weekend, I also met Jackie and Robin as well as several other individuals I felt a connection to. We visited while we were there, yet I truly had no indication of what would transpire in the months ahead. Returning home, four of us decided to commit to a weekly meet up designating a date and time to do so. While meditating at our respective locations, we would set an intention for each gathering. Although each of us was miles apart, we felt a very close connection for several months as we honed our gifts and shared with one another. Reflecting on this time together, I value and cherish it immensely. The bonds of friendship have been strengthened as we have supported one another through the endeavors we each undertake.

∞

Ros, and Friends from all over the World

The Facebook platform is a wonderful venue to connect with individuals literally all over the world. When I first joined Facebook a few years ago, I felt that the energy of the posts of my Facebook friends were very negative. I never posted anything as my status. I really didn't see the point of being on it. Having just a handful of friends at the time, my stomach churned when I would read what people had posted. I knew I didn't want to be any part of it. Apparently, I just needed new Facebook friends. Since I shifted my perception, I have now connected with hundreds of beautiful souls who choose to make a difference in the lives of others just as I do.

Through this venue, I have had the opportunity to connect with individuals all over the United States as well as in the United Kingdom, New Zealand, and Australia.

One such person is Ros. We met over two years ago and quickly became friends. Sharing similar beliefs and teachings, she asked me to post as her page while she was away on a retreat. Since connecting, we have spoken frequently sharing our experiences and spiritual journey with one another. Positivity abounds on her page as it does on many others that come to my immediate mind. Facebook enables Lightworkers a means to offer hope, love, healing and Light. In addition to having my own Facebook pages, my friends Sherri, Anthony, Jackie, and Robin, as well as many others I have not listed here, each have their respective pages and are assisting in raising the vibrations of individual and global consciousness as a whole.

∞

Lloyd and Melissa

Attending conferences and metaphysical fairs has provided me with opportunities to connect with people in my local area. In order to become a member of the Oklahoma Psychic Educational Research Association (OPERA), I was required to be evaluated by three members, so that I could offer readings and healing sessions at its metaphysical fair in Oklahoma City. I did a healing session for Lloyd, who was the fair coordinator at the time, and a reading for his wife, Melissa, as well as one other person. Based on their feedback, I passed with flying colors. I immediately felt a kinship and connection to them both. Offering healing and readings as well as intuitive drawings, Lloyd and Melissa emanate love and Light. I had the extreme pleasure of having my table next to these lovely souls at my inaugural fair.

Although I no longer participate in OPERA's metaphysical fairs, I recognize the importance of my participation. Lloyd soon created Starfield Press to publish his own works. As soon as I saw this, I knew with all of my heart that he would be the one to assist me with my own books. I am thankful for Lloyd's friendship and his dedication and service to Spirit. I was honored to have him format the eBook and print layouts, and create the beautiful cover design for this book, as well as *28 Days to a New YOU* and *Connect to the YOU Within*.

∞

Lana

In addition, I met my dear friend Lana at the OPERA fair. I was asked to be one of her testers, and I undeniably felt an immediate connection to her. The two of us regularly participate in Cyndy and Tammy's Spirit Fair together. Lana's wisdom and spiritual insight assist me greatly on my journey. Undoubtedly, we are in each other's life for a reason as well.

∞

Now that you've met some of the important people in my life and how they are a part of my journey into consciousness, let's continue this chapter with some talk about friendships and how these relationships help us on our spiritual journey:

Be a reflection of what you'd like to see in others! If you want
love, give love; if you want honesty, give honesty;
if you want respect, give respect.
You get in return what you give! ~ Unknown

The topic of friendship continues to come into my awareness. There are so many aspects I can focus on, but first, what is a friend?

According to the Merriam-Webster Dictionary.com, a friend is defined in four ways:

1. one attached to another by affection or esteem; an acquaintance
2. one that is not hostile; one that is of the same nation, party or group
3. one that favors or promotes something (as a charity)
4. a favored companion

To me, a friend is someone who is there for you when you need to talk. They will listen without judgment and offer advice when you ask (and even when you don't ask). They will tell you the truth even when you really don't want to hear the truth. There are also varying degrees of friendship. Typical terms are acquaintance, friend, close friend, dear friend, and best friend.

I prefer to think of my friendships with a solar system analogy. I am the sun in this solar system and each of my relationships are the planets — Mercury, Venus, Earth, Mars, Jupiter, Saturn, Uranus, Neptune, Pluto (yes, I still consider Pluto a planet).

Now, who would you consider your Mercury? This friend is the closest to you. They know everything about you, and they are your closest confidant. Then, who would be your Venus and so on? Pluto would be the casual acquaintances in your life. This analogy is simply a mental visualization especially since we all learned the phrase "My

Very Educated Mother Just Served Us Nine Pizza-pies" in school to learn the names of the planets. I believe you can have more than one friend in each "planet location," too.

Remember: The gifts of friendship can often be found in changes — even when friendships fade or end, the friendship is still part of us. It has contributed to how we are in the world and who we are as friends. ~ SARK

The resounding message, for most of our life, has been that people come into your life for a reason. It is not for us to determine what that reason is. There is no need to analyze the how, when, why, what, and where aspects of this interaction. Rather, I believe that we are meant to allow it to happen — allow the relationship to unfold and see where it takes us.

As the saying goes, "People come into your life for a reason, a season, or a lifetime." From my perspective, I recognize that it is not important for us to determine the particulars of the connection at the time it is made — whether the individual is in our life for a reason, a season or a lifetime. Only later, when the relationship has come to an end and ways have been parted, do we discover why. Simply enjoy each and every moment of the relationship during the time that it lasts.

It's important to see the blessings within the relationships that have ended rather than focusing on the outcome, as each encounter with another, offers us life lessons to learn from. Did this individual introduce you to someone else? Did this person offer you a lesson (an opportunity for learning and growth)?

The past few months I've had relationships with both friends and colleagues shift and change. It isn't a bad thing per se, it just happens. My friends know that I am always a phone call, text or email away if they need me. Some of my friends I am in daily contact with. Others, there may be days, weeks and even months that go by with very little contact, yet once we do talk; it's as if no time has passed. To me, that is what true friendship is all about. We are here to support, encourage, and love one another. Some people feel hurt and neglected if they have friends who aren't "daily connection" friends. When you feel this way, honor yourself and what you are feeling and then ask yourself a few questions. Have you reached out to those friends in your life? Have you let them know that you miss them or that you need them? Have you been the kind of friend to them that you want them to be? Friendship is most definitely a 2-way street.

The most beautiful discovery true friends make is that they can grow separately without growing apart. ~ Elisabeth Foley

I have had a few friends vocalize jealousy towards me. I recognize and "hear" what they are saying, but I also don't care for the jealousy/envy energy either. When this kind of thing affects me negatively, changes need to happen within the relationship. I honor what they are feeling and acknowledge the courage it takes to express these emotions. I feel that healthy communication is extremely important in order to have healthy relationships.

We are each having our own human life experience. For those believers in reincarnation (like me), our soul chose our life experiences prior to our incarnation, including the "good," the "bad," and the "ugly!" I love that each one of us is having our own experience on Earth school and that our lives intermingle. We are here to learn, to grow, and to evolve. As fellow travelers on this journey into consciousness, let's be happy for one another, celebrate the accomplishments, and be supportive during the challenging times.

These song lyrics from Dionne Warwick's song, *That's What Friends are For*, are speaking loud and clear to me in regards to seeing the blessings within the relationships that have ended and also cherishing those people who are in my life now:

Well, you came in loving me
And now there's so much more I see
And so by the way
I thank you
Oh and then for the times when we're apart
Well, then close your eyes and know
The words are coming from my heart
And then if you can remember
Keep smiling and keep shining
Knowing you can always count on me, for sure
That's what friends are for

In good times and bad times
I'll be on your side forever more
That's what friends are for

Songwriters: Allen, Peter W. / Bacharach, Burt F. / Cross, Christopher C. / Sager, Carole Bayer

Tell your friends what they mean to you.
Be the kind of friend you want in your life.
Don't take things personally.
Recognize that people change and so do relationships.

∞

The energy it takes to hang onto the past is holding you back from
a new life. What is it that you would let go of today?
~ Mary Manin Morrisey

Recently, I have found it extremely important to clear the clutter, so to speak, in my relationships. I have found it necessary to assess those relationships that are healthy and balanced and those relationships that are unhealthy and imbalanced (draining). I made the conscious decision to cultivate the healthy relationships and place some distance/establish boundaries in those relationships that I perceive to be unhealthy and imbalanced.

Attending a healing clinic in Eureka Springs, Arkansas in January 2012 set things in motion for me on many levels. I was listened to each and every word that was spoken, knowing with all of my being that these words were also intended for me.

On Saturday afternoon, I enjoyed a Soul Journeying session at Healthworks. The session was comprised of massage, intuitive energy work, aromatherapy, breath work, and sound therapy. The journey took me to the very depths of my soul allowing me to acknowledge what needed to be healed. At one point, the therapist asked me, "What are you so angry about? Why are you so frustrated?" I opened my mouth, and out it came, "I know that I am the only person that can make me feel this way, but sometimes I feel used and taken advantage of." Whoa! Did I really just say what I think I did? Yes, I said it, and it felt good to be honest. She said that I needed to receive as much as I give. That's where the problem lies. I am open to receiving, but I have always been the giver as the opportunity to receive does not seem to present itself.

Upon returning home, I was blessed with an offering to send me distant Reiki. For a moment, I wanted to question why, but instead this gift was gratefully received. The session was amazing, and I received the message, "Honor the Light within you." An hour later, I hosted my Blog Talk Radio show. This was the first time I had spoken to my guest. His voice was very kind, compassionate, and I would have to say angelic. I was guided to schedule a personal session with him afterwards as I was curious to see what he had to tell me personally. A very clear message involved the healing I still needed to do.

He stated simply with conviction, "You cannot appreciate the Light if you haven't gone through the dark." This is so true!

I have a savior complex. I tend to sacrifice myself and my own well-being, so that others do not hurt. I know that my experiences have enabled me to be a conscious counselor and more empathic to what others are feeling. During the reading, he went on to say, "Your soul chose this life, and you have to accept it. It happened to you, so you could help others." He said, "You always wonder why. Why not you? We are all here searching for unconditional acceptance. Your abusers were wounded long before they wounded you. As long as you hold onto where you were, you cannot get to where you are going."

The tears flowed, and I recognized what I needed to do next.

∞

The Universe is truly assisting me in becoming more aware of the intentions of others — love based or fear based (feelings of lack). I acknowledge that as I change, my relationships with others will change as well. I also recognize that the Universe is assisting me with changes in certain relationships in order for me to move forward with my work.

I invite you to join me in creating conscious connections with like-minded individuals who are walking the same path as you are. Ultimately, each one of us desires to be acknowledged, valued, appreciated, and loved. It is innate within each of us to love and to be loved.

Acknowledging my own gratitude, I am thankful for

the individuals who have come into my life and the experiences I have had. I am elated to think about the conscious connections I will be making in the future as well.

• 13 •
Stuck on Orbs

*We can then speculate that highly evolved Spirit Beings making
their presence known in orb photos will attempt to communicate
in any number of ways, including directing a message to the
person taking the photograph, delivering a message to the person
being photographed, or directing a message to a group of people or
even to mankind at large.*
~ Klaus Heinemann, Ph.D.

Orbs are emanations of Spirit.

MY FASINATION WITH ORBS BEGAN the moment
I noticed an orb on my head in a photograph taken with my
own Kodak Easy Share camera. This photo was taken at a
gazing event that I attended in Las Vegas, Nevada in
October 2010 with the Croatian healer, Braco. Since that
time, I began to pay attention as more orbs began to appear
in my photographs. Even going through photo albums, I
now see orbs that I did not previously see. I can say with all

degree of certainty that I would have noticed them and wondered what they were if they were there before. My only assumption is that my awareness is now heightened and my vision is clearer in regards to the Spirit realm.

In the ensuing months, I quickly became an orb "fanatic" and would take pictures quite often. Although I take photos indoors, my favorite location was outdoors after dark in a specific area of the yard between the house and my Reiki cabin. I would tell my family, "I will be right back," then step outdoors to see what or who I could capture. One night, my husband decided that he wanted to snap a few pictures for himself. This was the first and only time he has done so. Coming back in with a smile on his face, he captured some amazing pictures. I asked him what he said or if he said anything at all before he started taking pictures. Rather than telling me the words he spoke, he eluded that he made a specific request for a loved one to show his presence. He acknowledged that he received the validation he was seeking.

Since that time, my fascination with orbs has not subsided. Now, I just listen and follow my guidance. I will get that gentle nudge to head outdoors and start snapping away. I always gauge the weather conditions. It must be clear - no wind and not raining or snowing—to avoid possible dust or moisture in the air, which may cause doubt with the validity of the orbs.

When you pay attention and acknowledge the presence of orbs, you will be surprised at how often they will appear for you. Before taking pictures, I say aloud a prayer of protection, call upon my angels and guides, and start taking pictures. Sometimes, I see the orbs. Other times, I am just guided to turn and snap.

Some individuals may believe that orbs are dust particles or water marks. I choose to believe that they are emanations from Spirit Beings bringing forth messages of love and hope to mankind. I have chosen to share the orbs I have photographed as I feel that the messages they communicate are not only for me, but also for anyone who chooses to view them. In doing so, I have connected to a community of individuals who acknowledge and embrace orbs as well as the messages they bring.

During a segment on my Blog Talk Radio show in March 2012, I asked author and paranormal investigator, Larry Flaxman, for his take on the orb phenomenon. Larry is the President and founder of ARPAST, which is the acronym for Arkansas Paranormal & Anomalous Studies Team. According to the website arpast.org, "ARPAST is a science-based research group dedicated to furthering our measured understanding of anomalous and unexplained phenomena. Our goal is not to "prove" or "disprove" the existence of "ghosts" or "spirits." To carry such an agenda would be to presume an understanding of that which is not currently completely understood."

After posing the orb question, Larry paused and said, "I wish you would not have asked me that." Immediately, I had a feeling that he thought he was going to "burst my orb bubble." I assured him that I was curious and receptive to whatever he had to say. He said not once, but twice, "Don't shoot the messenger." He proceeded to discuss research conducted in an orb study subsidized by Fuji Film shortly after digital cameras became available. Due to the speed of the shutter, the imaging sensor and shutter speed of the digital camera are substantially faster and more sensitive than a regular 35mm camera; thus capturing air-borne particular matter, otherwise known as dust.

Larry proceeded to share an investigation story about seeing a blown up orb photo on the coffee table inside the homeowner's house; revealing he inquired about it and listened to the woman's interpretation. He noted that there is a humanity side to the paranormal work that he does and acknowledged that he is no better than anyone else, so he chose not to offer a scientific explanation to her.

Continuing, he indicated that human feelings are involved, and he is not going to tell someone who uses this tool as a grief coping mechanism any different. Plain and simple, Larry declared that everyone is entitled to their own beliefs. Finishing our conversation, I thanked him for his insight and revealed that I still believe in believing.

Who's to say that dust particles are not being used by Spirit?

A book titled, *Orbs: Their Mission and Messages of Hope*, written by Klaus Heinemann, Ph.D. & Gundi Heinemann notes:

1. Orbs are likely not Spirit Beings in and by themselves, but rather emanations from Spirit Beings.

2. Orbs show up of their own volition in digital photos and sometimes even in photos taken with conventional emulsion film cameras.

3. Due to the technology involved, it takes extremely little physical energy for an orb to be recorded in a digital photograph.

4. Orbs appear to take the minute amount of physical energy required for being recorded in digital images from the camera flash, or in a few cases, from other physical light or energy sources.

5. To minimize the energetic requirement for being recorded by cameras, orbs do not wastefully emit their (light) energy, but instead focus it with laser like accuracy into the camera rather than into other directions where there is no camera to capture them.

6. Orbs respond to requests to appear in photographs and will generally not bother showing up in photos when they anticipate their presence will not be noticed.

• 14 •
Awareness is Heightened

.

In the hopes of reaching the moon, men fail to see the flowers
that blossom at their feet. ~ Albert Schweitzer

Heightened awareness assists in
recognizing Spirit communication.

AWAKENING TO THE TRUTH OF who I am in 2008,
I began actively listening to the guidance I was receiving.
Paying attention to this guidance, I delved deeply into my
spiritual studies, and as I've already mentioned repeatedly,
Reiki played a defining role for me.

Awareness involves being conscious and utilizing your
five senses—sight, taste, touch, smell, and hearing.
Awareness includes being cognizant of your surroundings
and the people coming into and leaving your life. The
Universe will assist us in bringing people, teachers and
experiences into our awareness, so that we can learn, heal,
and grow. In order to begin heightening your own

awareness, it is essential to be mindful of all that you are experiencing in each and every moment. Incorporating enhanced awareness into your daily life will ultimately enrich your life.

For myself, I have noticed that certain people will come into my awareness at exactly the right time for me to receive a message. The message may not be directed specifically towards me, but I receive it loud and clear nonetheless. I can almost feel a switch being turned on and off enabling me to glean exactly what I need from the conversation. I recognize these as opportunities for learning and growth for myself.

In addition to the support network of our friends and family, each one of us has a guardian angel who has been with us since the moment we were born and will stay with us until we transition to the Afterlife. We also have access to the Archangelic realm and the Ascended Masters.

∞

WORKING WITH THE ARCHANGELS

Make yourself familiar with the angels, and behold them
frequently in spirit; for, without being seen,
they are present with you. ~ St Francis of Sales

The angels or celestial beings continue to remind us that they are with us standing by ready, willing, and able to assist. All we have to do is ask for their assistance as they cannot intervene in our free will choices unless the consequences are dire, and it is not our time to depart the earthly plane. We can call upon them for assistance at any time as they are available to everyone. You do not need to reference any particular Archangel or Ascended Master to receive support.

Simply say, "Archangels/Ascended Masters, I call upon you now!"

However, if you do wish to call upon a specific Archangel based on their specialties, I have provided a short list for you here. Please know that there are many others. I encourage you to seek resources to learn more about the Archangels and Ascended Masters. Doreen Virtue has written numerous books on this topic.

- Michael ~ strength, courage, determination, protection
- Raphael ~ healing
- Gabriel ~ communication
- Uriel ~ knowledge, understanding
- Chamuel ~ peace
- Ariel ~ manifesting
- Metatron ~ writing, achieving potential
- Azrael ~ transitions, healing
- Jophiel ~ beautifying thoughts, clearing clutter
- Raguel ~ relationship harmony
- Haniel ~ strengthening psychic abilities

Therefore, as an example, you would say, "Archangel Michael, I call upon you now. Please provide me with strength, courage and protection during this time."

For me personally, I choose to view the Archangels and their specialties as energetic archetypes. This energy is available to everyone at any time. All you have to do is ask. I regularly call upon the Archangels for assistance in my own life.

I am guided to mention that my Nanny has always had an affinity for angels. She has framed artwork and statues throughout her home. I didn't realize the significance of this until recently when I began sharing my spiritual journey with her.

∞

MEETING MY GUIDES

I believe we are free, within limits, and yet there is an unseen hand, a guiding angel, that somehow, like a submerged propeller, drives us on. ~ Rabindranath Tagore

Cultivating a relationship with your Spirit guides is beneficial and refreshing. The term Spirit guide refers to a non-physical entity that guides a soul through its many lives. I established communication with my own guides while doing the awareness exercises prior to the Intensive Mediumship workshop in November 2010 in Dallas, Texas. Some of my guides have left since that time and new ones have come in. This will happen because the journey we are on offers opportunities and experiences that may require new and/or additional assistance. My guides at that time were Raul, Fremanity, Currian, Kei Wei, Kiran, William and Samuel. I currently have Raul, Kei Wei, William, Prof. Jedediah Marshall, Davide, Cassie, Reginald and Kiran assisting me. As you can see, I have maintained four of the same guides. More than likely, as I continue on my journey into consciousness, I will have more guides leave and new ones step into help.

During a powerful Reiki share on December 7, 2010, images of several of my guides came through. When Kei Wei appeared, he was walking across a wooden bridge wearing wooden sandals and carrying a rod. He is Japanese and is my Reiki guide. Raul appears to be an older Cuban, and looks like the actor from the television show, *Fantasy Island*. Fremanity appeared to me as a wise older lady with long hair in a bun of European descent. She showed herself sitting in a rocking chair looking out a window. Currian is a Celtic female with red hair and is very calm, yet has a fiery attitude. Samuel is actually older and wise, but he said I could visualize him as young. He looks to me like the actor from the television show, *The Mentalist*.

While studying advanced mediumship with Lisa Williams, the course's exercises provided me with the motivation I needed to strengthen and cultivate the relationship that I have with each one of my guides. I recognize that they are patiently waiting for me to communicate with them regularly rather than rely on them periodically. I previously viewed them as a collective rather than separate entities. Now, I feel the tremendous need to recognize their individuality as each one has a purpose. Raul is my Master Guide; Kei Wei is my Reiki guide; William is my cheerleader/supporter; Prof. Jedediah Marshall, who insists on name formality, assists me with my writing; Davide assists me with relationships; Cassie is my Gatekeeper; Reginald is a peacekeeper/spiritual guru; Kiran works behind-the-scenes to assist the others.

I have opted to go into meditation on several occasions with the specific intent to learn more about each one of my guides. I chose to do so silently rather than using a guided meditation, although I have done that as well. My guides presented themselves to me one at a time, and I acknowledged their presence. As I continue on my personal journey into consciousness, I recognize that I definitely need to regularly spend time cultivating the relationship that I have with each one of them. My guides assist me daily in my work. Not only do they encourage my writing, but they are also my support team and biggest fans. Their loving guidance continues to remind me that affecting one person will have a ripple effect with many. I feel like it is important to mention that it is extremely comfortable, and minimal effort is required to connect with my guides. Doing so is as effortless as picking up the telephone to call a friend only no charges are incurred for making the connection. I can make the connection anywhere at any time. Please know that you are able to make this same connection with your own guides.

In October 2012, just before the Platform Mediumship class with Lisa Williams, my guide, Raul appeared to me. First of all, I should reveal that I've made it very clear to Spirit that I don't want to be scared or freaked out. With that being said, Raul comes into my visual awareness. I see him with my physical eyes as an energetic dot-to-dot profile. He only shows his face, and it is always facing to the left. Mind you, every time this happens, I smile and laugh. Whether I am going for a walk or driving in my car, his head will pop in and "float." At first, I thought he looked like the cartoon character Johnny Bravo; then I quickly realized he was wearing a turban with a jewel.

Each one of us has the ability to connect with our guides. You do not need a psychic or medium to do this for you. Simply set the intention during a meditation that you wish to connect with them. Our guides are less concerned with names and labels, and are excited for us to make the connection. Acknowledge the guidance you receive even though you may not understand it fully. Since you have free will, it is up to you to take action on this guidance.

∞

BRACO

My awareness became noticeably heightened after attending a gazing event with the Croatian healer, Braco, in Las Vegas, Nevada in October 2010. Just as the name suggests, gazing involves fixing your eyes and receiving a healing transmission without touch. Braco stands silently in front of the audience and gazes. The audience, in turn, gazes at him.

According to his website Braco.net, "Braco's gaze touches his visitors with peace, silence, and hope. Amazing transformations happen, and many find new power, vitality and a zest for life resulting from their experience. Braco does not teach, talk, or diagnose to give treatments — he simply gazes in silence and offers his gift to visitors — independent from religion, ideology, race, color and culture."

I gazed eleven times in the two days I was there and kept a journal of what I experienced:

October 12, 2010
1st gazing at 9:00 am on day one:

I saw the host's aura immediately and felt Jesus' presence. I felt washing, anointing and tingly during music. I could see Braco's aura. He looked like he had angel wings. I felt coldness up my right arm and my body swaying. I closed my eyes three different times to refresh them. I felt him looking right through me.

2nd gazing at 10:00 am:

This session was different. I saw Braco's aura and then his face change. It appeared like he had grown a beard. I held our family picture in my left hand over my heart. I felt pulsating energy in my right forearm. I also felt like he had a message for me.

3rd gazing at 11:00 am:

I drank water Braco had gazed at noting that it tasted thick, but sweet. I held the picture of my family. I felt throat action during the meditation. Braco looked like Jesus. I saw a beam of light coming down to a man's head in front of me, so I looked around to see if anyone else had one. I felt warm this time in my Heart Chakra. When the session was over, I spoke up and mentioned what I saw.

A lady behind me spoke up and said that is funny this happened because in the session before she saw my whole head and shoulders illuminated with white light. After the session, I was trembling full body. A lady in line told me it was God. I went to the bathroom and the lady who saw the light spoke to me telling me I was the only person that had this illumination that she had seen. The lady in line said a prayer and eased my trembling. Then, she spoke very kind words to me.

4th gazing at 12:15 pm:
During the meditation, I felt lots of activity in my Crown Chakra. When Braco came in, I felt grounded, yet had lots of pressure in my head. His face appeared half normal and half changed – unsure of what though. I almost wondered if I had too many sessions at once and then the pressure lightened.

5th gazing at 1:15 pm:
I felt swirling energy in my hands during the meditation. The energy felt peaceful. I felt lots of energy in my eyes at that time.

6th gazing at 2:15 pm:
Once again, this session felt different! I felt like a robe had been placed around my shoulders. I felt action in elbows and knees.

7th gazing at 3:15 pm:
I felt like I was glowing all over. I noticed action in my third eye and pineal gland at back of my head. I felt vibrations all over my body.

8th gazing and final for the day at 4:15 pm:
This session was termed a triple feature with music, Braco's recorded voice, and a gazing. I felt swirling energy all around my body. I felt prickly, tingly, warm, and joyful. I believe I will definitely get a message tonight!

∞

Once I returned to my hotel room, I decided to look at

the pictures in my digital camera from earlier. I noticed there was an orb on my head in the picture, so we looked at my friend's pictures as well. There was an orb in her picture of me, too. We decided to go take more pictures in hopes of capturing more orbs.

The following events ensued and were recorded in my journal:

We got in the elevator going down and the door would not open automatically. We did not hit any buttons and the next thing we knew we were on the 33rd floor. I remember looking at each other and wondering what just happened. We got out and walked around a bit taking pictures. We later discovered a really amazing image on one of the pictures – a light figure. We went to go back down and the elevator door opened with four firefighters in it asking us to please take the next one, so we did. We made it to the convention elevators. Two men and two women were staring at us and questioning what we were doing. We pressed convention floor, and they announced they were going to the 11th floor.

Making our way back to our room, a man smiled then pressed the elevator button. Four other people got in with us. The first person pushed button 21, I pushed button 22 and the third person pushed button 31. The elevator went straight to the 22nd floor skipping 21. This time, the others looked at each other wondering what had just happened. We simply smiled.

My friend and I got in our beds. In the darkness, I immediately saw purple, green and white sparkling energy above me. My friend saw it, too. I felt like I was melted to the bed. I felt sensations all over – feet washing, hand cleaning. It felt like I was undergoing a purification process. When I spoke the words, "I seal the room and let nothing but the white Light in," I felt intense pulsating energy all over.

I finally fell asleep and woke up at 5:45 am with bodily sensations again. I saw pictures of people as if I were walking down a hall and saw words, but could not make them out. Then, I saw a full picture like a postcard. It was a beautiful pink temple with blue and gold. The words "Be Blissful" were written in script along with some other words I do not remember. I fell back asleep and suddenly woke up at 7:38 am, waking up my friend to begin gazing once again.

This is what I noted in my journal for day two of the gazings:

October 13, 2010
1st gazing at 9:00 am on day two
I felt intensely warm and powerful energy. I saw Braco's aura and his face transformed to Jesus. I felt lots of energy in my hands.

2nd gazing at 10:00 am:
The opening music was powerful. I held our family picture. A woman told me I was sitting in a "seat of honor." The energy felt powerful, but different. It seemed to be integrating what was ingrained yesterday. My right arm twitched and jerked.

3rd gazing at 11:00 am:
The music was powerful once again. I sat further back by a woman, so that we could leave for the airport immediately after this session. I felt her energy during the music. I held the picture of my family. I felt powerful energy in my hands especially.

∞

After gazing that morning, it was time to catch a taxi and make my way back to the airport to return home. I shared a taxi with two very gentle, serene souls. One was the woman who spoke kind words to me the day before while I was trembling. Upon reaching the airport, I offered to pay the entire fare. One woman said I would have to ask the other in order to do so, which I did. I asked her if I could bless her and pay and she looked at me and said yes. Then she got out of the front seat and crawled in the back seat to hug me, kiss me on the left cheek, and tell me she loved me. I felt a deep connection to her and ultimately would be visiting her in just two weeks to learn Kriya yoga.

Arriving at the airport, I started feeling poorly. I was feeling hot and sick with a headache. I wasn't sure if I was having energy withdrawals or if I was feeling everyone else's energy at the airport. I began seeing people's auras (the etheric layer of the aura) after gazing with Braco.

∞

SIGNS

Heightened awareness also involves taking note of the signs that are being presented to us from the Spirit realm. Songs on the radio, television commercials, and even upcoming events brought into your awareness are worth paying attention to, especially if you keep seeing or hearing them repeatedly. Check in with yourself and assess if there is an underlying message or if you are intended to take it literally. Animal messengers and cloud formations, as well as anything else that catches your attention, should be noted. Symbols are everywhere and may mean one thing to an individual and something entirely different to another. Our perception assists us in our individual interpretation of these symbols. Sometimes, the message is not revealed to us immediately. Therefore, it is important to simply acknowledge the sign and not analyze it.

Practicing discernment and what feels right to you is essential. In doing so, clarity of the mental, physical and emotional bodies will occur. Silencing the mind chatter, communicating clearly, and becoming more aware will offer you this clarity. You will have a deeper understanding of your purpose here on Earth and will be renewed in every way if you allow yourself the opportunity.

∞

Signs have undoubtedly played an integral role in my ongoing spiritual evolution.

My daughter and I went on vacation together in July 2010 to celebrate my graduation from college—destination Disney World in Orlando, Florida. On the Southwest flight from St. Louis to Orlando, we selected our own seats. I spotted a girl with an outrageous Mohawk, wearing sunglasses, and covered in tattoos. Without hesitation, I decided we should sit by her. She was quiet (I later learned she had been sleeping), so I read my book, which was about synchronicity. After an hour, I put the book down, and she commented on the clouds and some of their shapes. Next thing I knew, we had this intense spiritual conversation. She is a singer and was on her way to Orlando to a recording studio. We covered everything possible in that period of time. I gave her the information for the book I was reading, and we exchanged emails. She told me that she knew we had known each other before, and that I would sit there. It was really an amazing experience.

∞

Once we got to the park, my daughter and I enjoyed ourselves and our time together. While we were waiting on the sidewalk for the afternoon parade to start at Magic Kingdom on Sunday, I looked up and saw a raven perched on the building in front of me. It began preening itself, and I watched three feathers float from its body. I knew that one was going to land right at my feet, and it did.

∞

Later that evening while we were waiting at a different spot on the sidewalk for the night parade, it started raining. I knew there would be a rainbow in the sky, so I kept watching in front of me. In one instant, I knew to look above and behind me and sure enough, there was a beautiful double rainbow.

∞

Probably the most amazing synchronistic event occurred at the airport in Houston on the way home. Our flight arrived twenty minutes early, so we went to the Life is Good© store and then got some nachos at Pappasitos. We sat at a table and about one minute later, the lady next to me asked if we had eaten at the pizza place before. I told her we really liked Pappasitos' nachos, and they didn't have them where we lived. She said that her mother had just passed away in May from an auto accident, and they would always eat at Pappasitos when she would go to the doctor. Then, she asked me where we were flying home to, and I told her. Her face changed and she said her older brother had been treated at the Cancer Treatment Center in Tulsa for eight months. She went on to say what an amazing place it was and asked me if I was familiar with it. I told her that I had heard of it and was actually thinking of contacting them to volunteer my services. I knew Reiki was one of the alternative healing modalities they utilized. She repeated to me several times that I should contact them because they could use me. I looked at my watch and told her that we needed to catch our flight, and she said that she did too. She told me once again to call them. I definitely took this to be the validation I needed to get in touch with the center, which I later did only to find out that they do not offer Reiki at the Tulsa location.

Rather than trying to interpret the meaning of these signs, I simply acknowledged them and expressed my gratitude for receiving them.

∞

A few months later, my husband and I were headed home from Kansas City after attending a class presented by Steffany Barton. I do not remember the name of it, but it was really powerful. He had to work the next day, so we made a quick round trip. Literally leaving the house at 2:00 pm, grabbing a quick bite at Panera Bread, and then getting to the church in time for her presentation from 7:00 - 9:00 pm; we subsequently left directly afterwards for the four-hour drive home.

We were about an hour away from home, and he was very tired, so we stopped for a break, and I told him I would drive. I knew he was really tired because he prefers to drive. I got into the driver's side of his truck and the seatbelt would not release, so I could put it on. I tried several times, and he said to take it as a sign. I got back in on the passenger side, and they both released immediately. The rest of the ride home was really unusual for me as I kept seeing all kinds of symbols. When I finally got home and crawled into bed, it really intensified. I saw an amazing tapestry among other things. I called Steffany the next day and told her about my experience. She told me that I wasn't meant to drive and more than likely I was seeing images from the Hall of Records.

On December 2, 2010, my day began with a short guided meditation and pulling a card for myself. This day I opted to use Doreen Virtue's *Archangel Oracle Cards*. The card I pulled for myself was "Spread Your Wings!" with Archangel Ariel stating, "Do not hold back right now. The timing is perfect, and you are ready to soar!" I accepted the message, but could feel the doubt settling in to my humanness. Truthfully, I questioned my abilities and my purpose.

A few hours later, I walked down my driveway to get the mail. I clearly remember the bright cloudless blue sky. Walking back up the driveway and nearing the house, there was one cloud in the sky. I stared at it in amazement and smiled. The image from the oracle card was being presented to me "bigger than the sky." I ran into the house, grabbed my camera, and snapped a few photos. I went back inside to upload it to my computer. Returning outside to view the cloud once again, it was completely gone.

Now I should mention that there are naysayers when I tell this story. They say it was the trail left behind by an airplane. To me, the how or what does not matter. The Universe provided me with a sign. I promptly recognized this sign and expressed my gratitude for it. This cloud picture is my inspiration to continue to spread my wings and soar and to encourage others to do the same.

∞

My family and friends are a significant part of my life, and they are incredibly important to me. I had the honor of reconnecting with a childhood friend in a truly remarkable way. I must begin the story with laying the groundwork, so that you will understand the significance of the story in its entirety. I will avoid most of the details and allow you to read between the lines.

I was awakened in the middle of the night in October 2011 with the imperative message of finding a new doctor. My doctor had closed her practice the previous year. I got online the next day finding a couple of specialists in the Tulsa area and was guided to contact one center in particular. Although the business name did not resonate with me, I called anyway. I indicated that I did not have a doctor preference and took the first available appointment.

I got there and the energy of the facility was truly awesome. It felt very relaxing and peaceful. I was escorted to the back by the nurse and immediately noticed that they didn't stop to weigh me. This was really favorable, in my opinion, as weight is a label of measure. The doctor came in shortly. She was so nice, and I connected to her immediately. She really listened to my answers; not half-listening like some physicians do. I had her complete undivided attention for about thirty minutes.

Coming back in to the room, she placed her hand on my back to listen to my heart with the stethoscope, and I knew immediately that I knew her. She asked me what I did for a living. I replied with some hesitation, "Well, I practice Reiki, which is energy work, and I am an Intuitive. I also do the books for my husband's business." She responded without judgment and mentioned a local city. It clicked. I immediately got her last name in my head. I was trying to decide how I should handle this. Should I freak her out and just say her name aloud? Instead, I smoothly asked her what her maiden name was. She told me and then immediately asked me if we went to high school together.

It was happening really fast. I told her that she probably wasn't going to believe this, and I provided her with my maiden name. She squealed loudly and started crying. I was crying too. She told me that she had just mentioned my name the week before to her mother while she had been looking at yearbooks. She wondered where I was and what I had been doing the past thirty-something years.

We hugged and hugged and cried some more. She was my best friend in the second grade. I moved away with my family to Denver, Colorado for a year before moving back to a different city in Oklahoma. I had thought about her from time to time, but never put forth the effort to find her. I truly believe we were destined to reconnect on that specific day. A few minor health issues were detected and subsequently resolved. We rekindled our friendship and the timing could not have been more perfect.

∞

DIVINE APPOINTMENT

I attended world-renowned author, vibrational healer and six sensory spiritual teacher Sonia Choquette's The Power of Your Spirit retreat at Unity Village in Lee's Summit, Missouri on August 24-25, 2012. I had been thinking about attending this retreat when it first came into my awareness in April, and I finally booked it on May 5. For whatever reason, I knew that I needed to attend. Arriving at Unity Village, I checked into the hotel and was given room number 407.

Of course, I looked at Doreen Virtue's book Angel Numbers 101 as soon as I got home to read the following message:

> 407 ~ *Heaven is giving you a strong sign that you're heading in a positive direction. Keep going!*

Making my way to the room, I noticed plaques positioned below the room number. I made it a point to read all that I passed. The plaque by my door stated, "May this room bring you inner Peace and God's special blessings. In loving memory of our parents..." What a beautiful message to be greeted with upon my arrival. I found myself smiling and feeling extremely joyful as I ventured outdoors to enjoy the beauty of the grounds. This was my first visit to Unity Village and the expansive serenity was palpable.

Friday night's interactive public presentation was delightful. I was especially grateful to my friend, Anthony, for offering me the gentle reminder to be prepared to dance because Sonia likes to dance. Thankfully, I knew to expect mobility! Waking up on Saturday morning, I was excited to see the unfolding of the day's events. We started the day with Sonia's "Breakfast of Champions" and began allowing our Spirit the opportunity to speak. She quickly encouraged us to name our Spirit, and I immediately got the name Penelope in my mind noting that I've name my mind chatter Nancy.

Pairing off into groups of two to four people throughout the day for the many exercises offered the opportunity to meet and connect with many of the attendees. Sonia also insisted that we keep changing seats. Early on and several times throughout the day, she made it clear that we had a Divine appointment to be here. Undoubtedly, I knew this to be true to the core of my being.

The retreat was infused with music – singing, dancing and allowing our Spirit to move. I continue to hear Sonia say, "How moveable are you?" She provided us with tools for our spiritual tool belt and offered a safe space for sharing and healing. Even now, I am continuing to bask in this experience and have integrated these new tools into my daily life and work.

The exercise "Digging for Gold" was extremely powerful. She invited us to speak aloud to our partner in this exercise, "If I wasn't afraid, I would _____." The words, many of them surprising to me as I heard them with my own ears, just poured from my mouth.

The words from her song, Love your Life, reverberate in my mind: *Dance your own dance. Sing your own song. Do your own thing. Love your own life....Sing your song.*

Yes, I am dancing my own dance and singing my own song!

My perception has shifted once again, and I love my own life...

∞

DREAMS

Through our dream state, awareness becomes heightened and our connection to Spirit becomes stronger. Some individuals believe that our dreams hold the key and offer insight to many areas of our life. My dreams are extremely vivid to the point that I sometimes question the reality I am in – if I am awake or dreaming. I also know that I astral travel while sleeping. Astral traveling is our soul's ability to travel on the astral plane. Yes, that means leaving our body while we are sleeping. We do not cross over because of our silver cord, which connects our physical body to our soul and is literally our lifeline.

Unable to actually verify my astral travel, an out-of-body experience or OOBE was verified for me by my husband on January 1, 2011. I woke up that morning to him asking me if I wanted to hear about his dream. Then he said, "Well it wasn't really a dream, but it was about you."

He then described what he saw:

I woke up hearing giggling and whispering. I reached over and felt in the bed wondering why you were up and talking on the phone so late. I saw the red button on the phone in the air. I opened my eyes and saw a transparent you above your body. I could see through you and saw the stuff hanging on the wall. I knew I wasn't dreaming because my eyes were wide open. Then, I saw the phone hang up and the transparent you go back into your body just like you were getting into bed. Then, your body started moving.

I remember waking up to use the bathroom, but had no recall of what had just transpired. I have received validation that I do leave my body at night.

There have been a few instances when I have awakened dizzy with the room spinning; I knew that I didn't quite make it back into my body properly. I would reach for my river rocks to ground—breathing in deeply and exhaling; then shutting my eyes to leave, so that I could try again. The first time it happened, I had no clue what to do. I assure you that it didn't take me long to figure it out.

Knowing that I should regularly keep a dream journal to record my dreams, I only do so on occasion. However, I have included some dreams in my mediumship journal in an upcoming chapter. I definitely dream in color. Some are even precognitive dreams offering me the ability to know something before it happens. I typically am not aware of the precognition dream association until the event does occur. Nonetheless, I thoroughly enjoy my nightly dreams and travels.

∞

Additionally, I definitely "sleep like a rock" and with rocks. I have a bowl of crystals by my bed, and I choose nightly which ones will make their way under my pillow. Crystals have powerful energetic properties. They can be used as psychic protection, to clear and balance chakras, as psychic tools and for healing. Each crystal has its own specific healing attributes. Although I can identify many crystals and their healing properties, the mass of my crystal collection has been acquired by listening to the guidance I receive. Simply speaking, I know when a crystal needs to come home with me. In addition to having crystals on my nightstand and under my pillow, they are also in my office and Reiki cabin. I meditate with crystals as well.

• 15 •
Offering Guidance to Others

*Every time you don't follow your inner guidance, you feel a loss
of energy, loss of power, a sense of spiritual deadness.*
~ Shakti Gawain

**My purpose is to assist others on their journey into
consciousness by empowering them to recognize and
acknowledge the guidance they are receiving
for themselves.**

Naturally, it seemed appropriate that
the next progression would involve me offering guidance
to others. I began offering readings using angel oracle cards
as divination tools to assist me. I first gave readings to my
friends. This eventually led to sharing messages on my
Facebook pages. Ultimately, I began to offer readings, with
the intention to read for others the way I would want to be
read for myself.

No one instructed me on which deck to select or even

how to use the cards. I listened to my inner knowingness and dove right in. My favorite deck to use is Doreen Virtue's *Healing with the Angels* oracle cards. The cards have an image and one or two words. I use these words as a prompt or cue to receive the message. The daily messages I offer on my Facebook pages derive from this particular deck. In addition, I also typically use Doreen Virtue's *Archangel Oracle Cards* and *Angel Therapy Oracle Cards*. Both of these decks are beautifully illustrated and have a message printed on the card. Each deck has a booklet enclosed with detailed meanings for each of the cards. I choose to follow my own intuition and guidance rather than refer to the booklet. In addition, I typically forgo any type of card spread. I simply shuffle the deck, listen to how many cards I should pull, turn them over and begin reading. Whenever a card jumps out or falls out while shuffling, I pay extra attention to the message as I know the angels want to make sure that it was received as well. In my opinion, there is no right way or wrong way when working with oracle cards – only your way. When choosing a deck and receiving a message, discern what feels right to you and follow your own intuition and inner guidance.

∞

Intrigued with Sherri Cortland's method of channeling information from her guides through automatic writing, I sought her advice on how to begin doing this as well. On July 21, 2010 my foray into automatic writing began using Sherri's prayer of protection and instructions. Absolutely nothing happened the first two times I attempted to write. I think I was trying too hard and thinking too much. On the third day, I could feel energy in my hand. Releasing the need to have control, I allowed my hand to move. Scribbles came through at first. Then, words that ran together.

A guide at the time, Fremanity, came through first. She

obviously had a sense of humor. Her writing was extremely tiny. I asked her to write bigger, so that I could read what was written. The word bigger appeared next. I laughed and said could you please write bigger, and so the word bigger appeared again, but this time the size was a little larger. Pretty soon, the words were large enough, so that I could read them. As I previously mentioned, the words initially ran together, and it was somewhat difficult for me to read what I had written. Since then, the words are spaced, but typically the t's are not crossed, the i's are not dotted and there is no punctuation. Nonetheless, I can easily read what has been written on the paper.

Some of the early messages were very short yet powerful:

Follow your heart and it will come.
Yes, live your life to the fullest.
Clieme [climb] time is now

Reading through my first journal, on 9/30/10 Fremanity offered me this advice:

Believe in yourself
Believe in others
Believe in God
Believe in Believing
Go for it all
Fremanity

Dedicating time daily to write, on October 5, 2010, Jesus came through and wrote:

See all of ourself. See one another of ourself.
See one another as love only love.
Feel love as energy. Feel love as love energy.
Be love love love

Love one another as you shall love yourself.
Jesus

You can imagine the look on my face as I read the word "Jesus." Questioning the practicality of such a possibility, I asked if this is THE Jesus and it was. The notion that Jesus would appear and offer me a message seemed remarkable and unrealistic to be honest. As an Ascended Master and teacher, Jesus is available to each of us, and this experience was a lesson for me to trust what I receive from Spirit.

On October 6, 2010, the message from Jesus was much longer:

Have faith and know that it is me you are speaking with. I know that you doubt yourself, but it is true. It is me. Believe and you shall see. I am here to tell you great things and you will be amazed at what unfolds. Hold true and be delighted. I am here to guide you and teach you. I have been waiting for this time to come and it is here my child.

Listen closely. I will share with you many stories. Know this to be true. Your journey is just beginning and I will be there with you. You will understand in due time. Do not question yourself or your abilities.

Live joyfully and abundantly as everything is taken care of always. You are kind and caring. Someone who loves everyone. Stay strong. Have faith. Be present. I will teach you many things. Love one another as you shall love yourself. I am love and you are love. We are love together. And so it is.

∞

As I was going through my journals, the following powerful messages came through in readings I did for others. I didn't ask at the time who was giving the messages and did not note who they were for as they were intermingled among other writings in the journal. Rather than assuming and assigning a name, I am noting the messenger as unknown. I am guided to share these wise words with you now.

- Start writing. Let go of the past, so that you can move forward. Live your life for you!
- Have faith. Do not seek the solution. Allow it to unfold.
- The road has been rocky at times, but is becoming easier to navigate.
- The world is your playground. See the beauty in everything and in all situations.
- Breathe the breath of life into your lungs. Rejoice in the knowledge and bestow this knowledge to your children.
- Have no fear, let go of worries, and see love everywhere for love is all there truly is.
- Lighten your load and heal your heart.
- Pay attention to the small stuff, but don't sweat the small stuff.

∞

My first official public outing for offering readings was the 2011 Ozark Mountain Publishing Transformation Conference in Rogers, Arkansas. I had a booth and offered Reiki as well as Reiki-related items for sale. I met the then-President of OPERA (acronym for Oklahoma Psychic Educational Research Association) at the conference. I had no idea that this association existed and promptly made application to become a member. According to operaok.com, "This corporation is a non-profit, educational, research association devoted to the study of art and science of the energies and universal laws governing the holistic relation of mind, emotion, body and spirit."

I worked my first OPERA metaphysical fair in August 2011 after passing my membership evaluation and continued working the scheduled fairs for the next year. In addition, I discovered Cyndy and Tammy's Spirit Fair as well as a holistic fair after both came into my awareness. Each of these fairs offered me an opportunity to shine my Light and share the love by offering Reiki and guidance to others.

∞

At the October 2011 OPERA fair, I began letting my human-ness cloud my Light. I set up my table Friday night just as I did in August. I also had the honor of evaluating an individual for membership to read at the next fair. I arrived Saturday morning ready to work and felt really good about the day and the connections I was making. I presented my talk, "Life Enhancement: Assisting you in Empowering YOU!" at noon to the attendees. Since OPERA's mission involves education, the fair includes free lectures running the gamut of topics. Speakers are invited to submit their topic in advance to be listed on the schedule as the number of presentations is limited due to time constraints.

Sunday afternoon arrived, and I began wondering if the services I offered were the "right" ones — meaning the services individuals are seeking. Doubt will creep in and rear its less-than-desirable-head on occasion. I wondered if I was even supposed to be doing this work. Now, I realize this is the ego or human-ness getting in the way.

I quickly silenced the mind chatter and told myself as I always encourage others, "You are exactly where you are supposed to be at this moment doing exactly what you are supposed to be doing."

As an Intuitive Medium, I have quickly realized that my purpose extends further than offering immediate answers as I believe I am supposed to assist others with their transformation by providing tools for people to access the information for themselves.

I prefer to call myself an Intuitive because the energy of the word, in my opinion, is conducive to acceptance and openness. I recognize that I have psychic abilities, yet do not like to label myself as a Psychic. For clarification purposes, "Psychic" means of the soul, and an "Intuitive" is utilizing your sixth sense or intuition. Everyone has a sixth sense and is capable of developing their intuition as well as psychic abilities.

A medium is an individual who has the ability to communicate with the Spirit realm using psychic abilities and is a channel for Spirit. Mediumship is the term used to describe a medium's work and involves receiving the information through the five senses and then conveying it to the client, so that they can understand. It is all about perception. The reader receives and perceives the information and then conveys it to the client. The client then perceives what is being conveyed. All Mediums are Psychics, but not all Psychics are Mediums.

As an Intuitive Medium, I utilize all of my psychic abilities, including claircognizance, clairsentience, clairvoyance and clairaudience.

Please note the following definitions for each term:

• Claircognizance, also known as clear knowing, is the ability to know things without having to be told.
• Clairsentience, also known as clear feeling, is the ability to tune into another person's emotional or physical sensations.
• Clairvoyance, also known as clear seeing, is the ability to see Spirit within the mind's eye or externally.

• Clairaudience, also known as clear hearing, is the ability to hear voices and other noises, either as an external sound or within a person's mind.

A mediumship reading offers you the opportunity to connect with loved ones in Spirit as well as receive guidance from your angels and guides. There is no guarantee that the loved one you wish to connect with will come through. As I connect to the spiritual realm, I convey the messages to you exactly as I receive and perceive them. Through this connection, my intention is to help you heal, grow and become empowered. I request and intend that the messages are conveyed to me clearly and accurately, and that I receive messages that are easy to understand for your highest good.

I am primarily clairsentient and claircognizant. I have spurts of clairvoyance and clairaudience, and I keep asking for my guides and angels to assist me in opening these psychic senses. I recognize that I am supposed to be patient, trust and accept that knowing is enough. In the beginning, my human side (ego) would try to make me doubt the information I was receiving. I wanted the audio and video to go with it! I also had to release the preconceived notions of what I thought Spirit communication would be like. Many times it is very subtle, which is why it is necessary to have heightened awareness in order to detect this communication.

When working with clients, I will feel on areas of my body the places I need to focus on and mention. Once I verbally express it (acknowledge), then I release it mentally as not being mine (release). It takes practice, but becomes easier to recognize.

∞

I am very adamant about not being a fortune teller and offering people definitive timelines or events for their future. I do not want to take the fun and excitement out of the unfolding. Coming from a place of respect, truth, integrity and love, I honor your free will and recognize that you are co-creating your reality with the Universe. Therefore, I am not a fortune teller and will not predict your future.

I have made this very clear during *The Shelly Wilson Show* on Blog Talk Radio. In the show introduction prior to opening the phone lines for callers, I spell this out for the listeners. Frequent listeners know what to expect when they call in to ask a question. New listeners are taken off guard because they are not sure how to phrase their question after hearing the introduction. When offering guidance to callers, I listen to the question being asked as well as the wording used, manner in which it is expressed and the energy of the caller and question. Rather than simply providing guidance, I provide tools to assist them on their journey. I believe, as a teacher, that knowledge is the key to unlocking the door.

∞

Offering guidance to others requires that I keep my emotions intact. I will pause, breathe in deeply, and focus on being present. I open my heart to love and choose to speak with compassion and kindness. I find myself speaking slower and softer when my client becomes emotional. I am receptive to their emotions and am able to discern the appropriate reaction noting that it is many times necessary to have no reaction. I have also learned to detach after giving the reading. I realize that I can only give what I get; it is my perception and interpretation of what I receive and then convey; it is the client's perception of what they are receiving; and finally, some people are simply unhappy. Nothing I say is what they really want to hear.

∞

TRUST

A lesson in trust occurred while working Cyndy and Tammy's Spirit Fair in Tulsa in October 2011. Saturday morning, as I was preparing to leave the house to drive to Tulsa, I decided not to wear my Labradorite necklace that I normally wear when attending fairs. I opted instead to bring a stone to carry in my pocket. According to *The Crystal Bible* by Judy Hall, Labradorite "raises consciousness and connects with universal energies, deflects unwanted energies from the aura and prevents energy leakage as well as forms a barrier to negative energies shed during therapy."

As I began setting up my table, I realized that the stone was no longer in my pocket. I retraced my steps thinking that it had fallen out. I could not find it, and I immediately chose to view the experience as a learning one. I decided that I needed to let my guard down and not be so protective; allow myself to just BE—knowing that all is well. As the healers, readers and vendors joined hands in circle prior to the opening of the fair, a fellow reader offered this suggestion to each one of us. His message was to "let our guards down and allow the chaos to come in"—cleaning house, so to speak. His words validated the message I received for myself after losing the stone.

After doing a few readings and offering life enhancement suggestions, I had a family of three make a request to connect to their loved one. Please bear in mind that my signage did not indicate mediumship. This experience was "my test" of stepping outside of the box—the box that I had made for myself limiting the services that

I offer. An hour or so later, another individual came to me requesting to connect to their loved ones as well. On Sunday, another individual wished to connect to their pet. I had three experiences as validation that I should expand into mediumship work. I could feel the path I was on was shifting. I was uncertain as to what my exact calling was in that moment. My guard was down, the walls of the box were gone, and I could feel: I AM creating my life!

As a side note, during a session with a client in January 2012, he handed me a large Labradorite crystal. He said he didn't know why, but he was guided to bring it to me as a gift. I just smiled because I knew exactly why.

∞

COME FROM A PLACE OF LOVE

I recognize that I simply need to just give what I get rather than doubting myself. It is a matter of getting out of my own way. I need to quit trying to control my journey and simply allow it to unfold as it should. Each one of us needs to be present, express our gratitude, and enjoy the ride. We need to get out of the way and allow the miracle of our life to unfold before our eyes. We need to trust and have patience in the process. And most of all...we need to love and live our lives fully without regret.

In the fall of 2011, I began using the phrase, "Sharing the Love" in my posts on Facebook. I use it when I offer complementary readings and when I am expressing gratitude to others for sharing my pages. However, this simple phrase means much more. I believe it is an expression of love as well as an expression of gratitude that reaches and expands far greater than the Facebook platform. I always envision my hand outstretched, or my arms wrapped around another giving them a hug when I use this phrase.

The following quote has always spoken to my heart:

To the world you might be one person, but to one person
you might be the world. ~ Author Unknown

Love is a feeling, an emotion, a state of being. How can one truly share love? One can share love by several means—being kind, smiling, offering an ear to listen, having compassion, being considerate, and assisting another. Through loving one another and projecting this love energy into the Universe, we raise the vibration of ourselves and humanity as a whole. Let us all take the time to share the love with one another and truly mean it.

∞

I AM A PSYCHIC

As I continue to move forward, my path is changing and I am beginning to own the label Psychic. Spirit is helping me to shift my perception of the word's connotation. My dear friend, Lana, gently but sternly told me that I needed to own who I am. She said, "Girl, the word intuitive is for babies. You need to own the power." I smiled and laughed as she always has the perfect way to convey a message to me. She was simply saying that psychic abilities are gifts that should be acknowledged and appreciated rather than understated with a word that is more comfortable. For now, I am going to continue to refer to myself as an Intuitive Medium. I've got to ease into this change. I am definitely not afraid, but recognize that I will be ready to make the switch when I am supposed to. My guides have lovingly been giving me daily "hits" (pieces of information), and I have been immediately acting upon them. I have to say that I am thankful that I do.

• 16 •
Journey Into Mediumship

The day which we fear as our last is but the birthday of eternity.
~ Seneca

Our loved ones in Spirit are with us.

ONE SUNDAY MORNING IN JANUARY 2010, my journey really began to shift. I was guided to purchase the Tulsa World Sunday newspaper. Living an hour from Tulsa, I seldom (and I mean seldom) buy the paper to read. I flipped through the entertainment section, and there was an ad indicating Psychic Medium Lisa Williams would be in Tulsa at the Performing Arts Center on February 2, 2010. I didn't know who she was, but I knew that I had to be there. I promptly got online and purchased two tickets. I attended the event with my husband and LOVED it! I immediately came home, purchased Lisa's book, and signed up for her newsletter online. Signing up was essential as this is how I later learned about her Intensive

Mediumship Course offered in Dallas, Texas in November 2010.

Before proceeding any further, I would like to define the practice of mediumship.

WHAT IS A MEDIUM?

A medium is an individual who has the ability to communicate with the Spirit realm using psychic abilities. There are two types of mediumship—physical and mental. Physical mediumship involves something physical happening that can be seen or heard by others, such as rapping, ectoplasm, and transfiguration. This evidence requires more energy from Spirit to produce. Mental mediumship involves relaying the information that you receive through sight, taste, smell, hearing and feeling. The differences between the two types are just as their names imply. Physical involves producing evidence that someone else can see; therefore, it is somewhat tangible or is at least witnessed by another. Mental relies solely on communicating the information you receive. Therefore, mediumship is the term used to describe a medium's work.

Mediumship involves receiving the information through the five senses and then conveying it to the client, so that they can understand. It is all about perception. The reader perceives the information and then conveys it to the client. The client then perceives what is being conveyed.

When describing mediumship to someone who has not experienced it before, I begin by telling them that the Spirit realm, also known as the Other Side, is literally right here all around us and illustrate this by extending my arm upwards at an angle. Our loved ones no longer have a physical body and are vibrating at a higher frequency than the earthly plane. Lastly, I explain how I typically receive the messages and the manner in which I do so. When communicating this information, I rely on my intuition and choose my words mindfully based on the reaction of the client – both verbally and nonverbally.

∞

In July 2010, I received Lisa Williams' newsletter indicating that she was holding an Intensive Mediumship Workshop in Dallas, Texas. I immediately filled out the information and had an undeniable knowing that I would be selected for the course. I submitted my application and waited to hear a response. A week or so went by, and I received confirmation that I was accepted to attend. Delighted, I immediately made my flight and hotel reservations and was eagerly looking forward to the class in November.

Lisa created an event on Facebook and possible participants joined upon making application indicating that they would be attending. Through this event posting, I connected with several fellow attendees on Facebook prior to the event. As the class time approached, Venice posted on the wall seeking someone to share a hotel room with. I thought about it for a moment, and realized that we shared the same birthdate after looking at her Facebook profile. I took this as a sign from the Universe to accept and room together that weekend. In addition to sharing the hotel expense, this would be an opportunity to make a conscious connection.

Lisa provided us with some suggested lessons prior to attending the workshop, and I diligently completed each and every one of them. I intended to take this course very seriously. I am guided to share my journal with you, so that you can observe a glimpse of what I experienced in the days prior to the class.

Intensive Mediumship Journal

October 20, 2010

I found it difficult to sit still in silence during meditation. I normally listen to guided meditations. I saw red, orange, and purple energy. I heard the words "be still" in my head.

October 21, 2010

Between 7:06 am and 7:30 am, while lying in bed, I felt like my body was paralyzed and I could not speak. My body seemed to be levitating, and I heard a female voice chattering in my right ear. I spent time in meditation this evening, and it was easier to be still. I spent some time sitting upright and the remainder of the time flat on my back. I could feel sensations in my hands, feet and down my spine. I saw lots of energy.

October 22, 2010

I did not have time to meditate as I was traveling. However, I meditated on the flight to Houston, Texas.

October 23, 2010

Today is Kriya yoga initiation. I spent a good portion of the day learning Kriya yoga techniques for different meditations.

October 24, 2010

I was visited by purple sparkling energy prior to falling asleep Saturday night. I spent two hours meditating in the morning and two hours in the afternoon. I meditated on the flight back to Tulsa as well.

October 25, 2010

I woke up and then remained still while meditating – all the while focusing on the sound in my head, the light in my third eye and the energy pulsing in crown. I went back to sleep.

October 26, 2010

I did the same as the day before. I am adjusting to the new energies since learning Kriya yoga. I had extremely vivid dreams.

October 27, 2010

Once again, I woke up and then lay still, relishing the sound, pulsations, and light show I was experiencing. I intend to call forth my angels and guides tomorrow to begin communication. I am adjusting to the shift since gazing with Braco in Las Vegas and the Kriya yoga initiation.

October 28, 2010

I asked my guides to come forward in this meditation. I used clear quartz and amethyst crystals. I lit incense. I saw purple pulsating energy infused with white sparkles, and felt coldness down my shoulders and spine. I felt lots of action on my Crown Chakra.

I began dialogue through automatic writing:

Who are you?

I am your friend Jesus.

How can you help me?

I can guide you in your work and help you to connect. This is my duty and I love you.

What is your purpose?

Guide you in your work.

Do you have a message for me?

Yes, I am so proud of you and all that you are and all that you will be. Your new life has begun. Listen to me when I speak to you. Hear my words and rejoice for it is time to get started. Many teachers will come into your life. Learn from them and teach others what you learn for it will help them. Know this and believe for it is so. Jesus

*Note: I felt that the message would come through more easily if I did automatic writing. Jesus first appeared during my writing sessions on October 5, 2010.

October 29, 2010

I ran errands in the morning. I decided to meditate lying down with an amethyst crystal on my third eye. I saw lots of sparkling energy and felt very relaxed. I immediately went to sleep for a nap and woke up feeling energized. I have felt tired in the past few weeks after traveling to gaze with Braco and learn Kriya yoga. I have either slept late or taken a nap each day. My dreams are numerous, detailed and vivid, having several during the night.

One dream involved seeing eggs with yolks inside. A few turned into chicks in front of me and broke through shells. The chicks then metamorphasized into white mice scurrying around. Then, they turned into little brown squirrels and were leaping and jumping around.

*Note: I found this dream to be quite fascinating, so I looked in Ted Andrew's *Animal-Speak Pocket Guide to Understand the Significance of the Animals*. After reading the descriptions, I immediately acknowledged the message of a new beginning, paying attention to the details and having balance in my life. Conveying this message in this manner was perplexing, yet definitely one that I will not forget.

Animal-Speak noted the following:

1) Chicken (fertility & divination) – This is a time of fertility in most areas of your life. Explore forms of divination to determine where best to place efforts.

2) Mouse (details) – Focus on the details. Attending to the little things will lead to bigger opportunities. Do not allow your attention to be distracted.

3) Squirrel (work and play) – Balance your work and play. Prepare for the future, but do not get lost in preparations. Find ways to gather and to gift.

October 30, 2010

I listened to fifteen minutes of Kriya yoga meditation and then sat quietly for the remainder of time. I felt pulsating and saw energy. My food cravings have reduced. I find myself eating less during the day. I had vivid dreams.

I wrote through automatic writing:

Who are you?
I am your guide William.
How can you help me?
I am your joy guide. I wish to make you happy and fulfill your dreams and desires.
What is your purpose?
I am with you and will assist you in your work. Call upon me to help you.

October 31, 2010
I sat in silent meditation. I felt tingly and saw energy. I worked outside in flower beds and enjoyed the fresh air and beautiful weather. My dreams did not seem as active last night.
I wrote through automatic writing:

Who are you?
I am your guide Currian. Yes, my name is Currian. I am your warrior guide. One who protects you at all times.
How can you help me?
I am here for you to call upon whenever you need assistance.
What is your purpose?
I am with you in your time of need.
*Note: I saw the profile of a cloaked individual in my third eye surrounded by white light.
I continued to write:

Yes, my name is Raul. I am your gate keeper. I am here to assist you in your work.
Yes, hello Shelly. My name is Samuel. I am here to help you as well.
Yes, my name is Jophiel. I am an angel of peace and love.
Yes, your work is unfolding. Listen carefully to my words. I am here for you. Raul

November 1, 2010

I felt rested and excited about the upcoming weekend in Dallas. I am looking forward to the experience. When meditating, I felt energy in my hands and down my spine. I felt a pulsating on my crown and saw lots of purple energy. I asked for loved ones in Spirit to come forward. I did not see or hear anything. I used a pendulum for the first time. I asked for my father-in-law and Pa to come through.

I wrote through automatic writing:

Currian is here for you. Now, so is Samuel and Raul. Ask us to help you call forth your loved ones in Spirit.

I asked Raul to help me bring forth my Pa, and I heard in my head, "It is not time." I felt cold down my shoulders and arms.

I wrote through automatic writing:

Currian says now is not the time. You are not ready yet. Jesus.

I then felt pressure in my head.

November 2, 2010

Wow! I had lots of dreams last night and this morning. I went back to sleep after my daughter left for school. My body and head feel like they are swaying. I decided to take pictures inside the house last night hoping to capture some orbs in the images. Orbs showed up in eleven out of twenty pictures I had taken. I sat for a short time and then decided to lie down on my back. I felt a sensation on top of my nose. My head felt like it was being held. I felt action in my right foot and tingling. I kept my eyes up staring upward for half of the time and saw energy moving and shifting, looking somewhat like a face. I do not feel like I connected with loved ones, but did feel a presence.

I wrote through automatic writing:

Follow your intuition, and I will guide you for it will happen in due time. The time is not right yet. Be patient. Jesus

Do not worry. Have faith. Be at peace with the process.

Jesus. *Shelly, believe in the process.*

November 3, 2010
I had lots of vivid dreams once again. I didn't recognize the places, but did recognize lots of the people. I woke up at 3:00 am and could not go back to sleep. I meditated lying on my back for one hour in silence with an amethyst crystal on my third eye. I saw lots of energy and flashes. I could see movement and people, but a gauzy curtain did not allow me to see clearly. I felt pulsing in my right ear and a fullness, but no sound.

I wrote through automatic writing:

Currian is here now. Yes I am with you. You should ask for Raul to help you. Raul is here. Yes, you will hear and see Spirit in due time. Be patient. Yes, feel me with you. I am here to help you now. Your Pa is not available at this time. Your father-in-law is here.

November 4, 2010
Once again, I had lots of crazy dreams. Some of these dreams seem to have been replays from another night. They were so familiar. I woke up at 2:00 am, but was able to go back to sleep. I am feeling a bit nervous about the upcoming class. I really need to boost my confidence.

I meditated for thirty minutes lying on my back with an amethyst crystal on my third eye. I saw lots of swirling energy with both my eyes closed and my eyes opened. I am hoping for the breakthrough today. I felt pulsing energy and could hear "waves," but not words. Perhaps, I am trying too hard. I feel pressure in my head and at the base of my neck.

I wrote through automatic writing:

Yes, Shelly. Be patient and have faith. There is no time like the present, but as you say, timing is everything. Your loved ones will come through. Relax. Have confidence. Rejoice in the unfolding. Call upon Currian and Raul to help you now. Jesus

November 5, 2010

I feel much better today! I had lots of awesome dreams. One dream was that I was on a ship in rough water; then navigating up a channel to dry land. I had another dream where I was doing Kriya yoga in a room full of people I do not know.

∞

WORKSHOP

A few days prior to the workshop, I began having feelings of nervousness, inadequacy and insecurity. Whoa! I wasn't sure if I liked what I was feeling. Arriving in Dallas, I met with several other attendees, and they were feeling the same way too. The class started Saturday morning with Lisa immediately putting us all at ease. She emphatically proclaimed that she hand-picked each one of us for this workshop, and we were supposed to be there. She informed us that seventy-five participants out of several hundred applicants were selected to attend this course, and I have no doubt Spirit played a role in the selection process. I absorbed the information that Lisa presented to us. I was very curious to learn about life after death in more detail. To begin with, many people ask these questions seeking answers about their loved ones and their transition to the other side or Afterlife:

- Where are my loved ones?
- What are my loved ones doing?
- Can my loved ones see me?
- Are my loved ones with me?
- Can my loved ones hear me when I speak to them?

I learned about the transition process. When it is time to transition from the earthly realm to the Afterlife or Spirit realm, the individual's aura becomes weak, dull and colorless. In turn, this causes the silver cord to become weak and ultimately break - resulting in death of the physical body. The silver cord connects our physical body to our soul and is literally our lifeline. When the physical body dies, our soul is transported to the Afterlife by the etheric aura. Astral traveling is possible because we are still attached to our physical body via our silver cord.

After leaving the body, the soul moves toward the veil and then crosses over into the white Light. Some souls choose not to cross over and remain in the vortex, which is the area between the earth plane and the Afterlife. Those who cross over are met by their loved ones in Spirit. Feelings of peace, love, and serenity wash over them as they make this transition.

∞

The readings we did for one another that weekend pushed me out of my comfort zone, yet provided me with the confidence to recognize that I am capable of being a medium. During one group exercise, I looked around at my fellow group members and didn't say very much. I knew that I didn't want to be the one to wear the blindfold and give messages to the group. Robin was sitting on my right side, and I remember staring intently at Anthony, in particular. The two of us never exchanged words during the weekend, but came home and immediately connected. As I stated before, we encourage and support each other personally and professionally, and I am thankful for his friendship.

I initiated a "Reiki share or whatever" gathering in my hotel room both Saturday and Sunday nights. I was guided to invite anyone who would like to join us and share whatever they desired. We had quite a spiritual party going on those two nights sharing Reiki, readings and fellowship with one another. It was truly an amazing time.

One of the participants summed up the experience in this manner, "The 'after intensive' experiences in room 522 were very auspicious because no one really knew what might happen. We were so open and so willing for true Light to embrace and energize us that only magical things could happen; and they did."

Those evenings truly were enchanting and were the inception of my friendship with Robin. She made the choice to participate in the gathering and this was just the beginning of what was to come. I feel Spirit was pleased with our willingness to be open to the experiences that occurred and this was setting the stage for our future work.

∞

The weekend ended and a group of us began a weekly meet up as I mentioned in a previous chapter. Although we were miles apart, we felt a very close connection for many months as we honed our gifts and shared with one another. Our time working together is one that I will truly cherish and never forget. The workshop served as a platform for creating conscious connections and was the catalyst for transformation in many of our lives. Lisa consistently instilled within each one of us throughout that weekend the importance of believing in ourselves and the work that we are doing. The words—respect, truth, integrity and love— continue to embody our journey.

• 17 •
Journey Into Mediumship - Part Two

For death is no more than a turning of us
over from time to eternity. ~ William Penn

Spirit communication can be very subtle
or quite apparent.
Our loved ones in Spirit use
whatever means available to get our attention.

FAST FORWARD A YEAR AND Lisa Williams was a
guest on my Blog Talk Radio show in December 2011. I
asked her if she would be offering another mediumship
class any time soon. She chuckled and indicated that she
had just put the course information on her website. To be
completely honest with you, I had been questioning if I was
supposed to be doing mediumship. I "hem-hawed" around
in December before I filled out the application; then turned
it over to Lisa and the Universe to decide for me. Within
twenty-four hours, I was accepted to attend her Advanced

Mediumship class. The class would be comprised of on-line webinars, homework, and a three-day weekend workshop in Calabasas, California in April 2012.

∞

Near the end of January 2012, I was thinking about my friend Robin when the phone rang and it was her. I smiled and immediately knew that she had something important to share. She wanted me to know that Psychic Medium James Van Praagh would be offering a five-day mediumship workshop in Seattle the next month and wanted to know what I thought about it. This was her way of feeling me out. As soon as she said it, I had this understanding that I needed to be there as well. Her exact words were, "I don't think we need to put all of our eggs in Lisa's basket." She meant that it would be a good idea for us to be trained by another teacher, so that we could extend our scope of knowledge. Within twenty-four hours of her call and after speaking to my husband, I enrolled in the course, booked the flight, and made hotel reservations.

During the week of February 13-17, 2012 in Seattle, Washington, one hundred individuals participated in an intense experiential Mastering Mediumship class for novice to advanced mediums and anyone interested in developing their intuition. For five days, James Van Praagh intently assisted those in attendance in a series of developmental and intuitive exercises to clear the mind and create a strong connection with the Spirit world. I can think of so many words to describe my week in Seattle studying mediumship. The truth is that I have found it somewhat challenging to actually use words to describe my experiences and to write about them. James is a compassionate, loving, and insightful man, yet he encouraged us to step out of the boxes we created for ourselves and "to not think—just do." James invited us to "own" what we "know." His method of instruction as well as his teachings and exercises is different than Lisa's, and I am thankful to Robin for her suggestion that we attend.

I met and worked with many wonderful individuals throughout the week as the Universe kindly made sure that we personally connected. In addition to the regular experiential workshop, James facilitated a Spirit development circle on Tuesday and Thursday night for those who wished to partake. Of course, I was not going to miss an opportunity for development. Each experience was unique, and I could feel a shift occur within myself.

During Thursday's class, we did physical mediumship involving transfiguration. Looking across at my partner, I could see half of his face change while the other half remained the same. I thought to myself, "Is this it? Is this all I'm going to see?" Well, the next moment Spirit made sure that I was amazed. In one instant, Spirit provided me with a clear-cut view of the Spirit realm. All I could do was smile and give thanks for this opportunity. To be completely honest, I was absolutely blown away with what I witnessed and experienced. The week exceeded my expectations. Any preconceived notions I may have had about the week "didn't hold a candle" to what actually occurred as I was in complete awe.

∞

At the time of this writing, I have known for some time that I am a medium and can do the work. Having the confidence to do mediumship is another story. I recognize these feelings and am working through them. I had turned these feelings over to the Universe and asked for a sign if I should do the work. As you may have guess, I got the signs I needed to forge ahead. Our ego emits doubt, and we must always trust in Spirit and allow ourselves to move forward.

∞

I started the online portion of Lisa William's Advanced Mediumship class in mid-March 2012 and began journaling at that time. Throughout the online portion, I learned a lot about myself. In that respect, I allowed myself to make some necessary changes in my life, specifically regarding establishing boundaries both personally and professionally speaking. I have included some excerpts from my journal. In doing so, I am offering you an inside glimpse, through my eyes, of what I was experiencing during that time.

∞

ADVANCED MEDIUMSHIP JOURNAL

March 26, 2012
During my special time this morning, my Pa visited me. My mind is still processing the dream visit. He passed nearly twenty-three years ago. I did not recognize where I was at, but he was sitting at a table telling me that he was going to stay with me, so that I could assist him and others in the Spirit realm.

March 27, 2012
I was just awakened at 5:44 am with a voice in my left ear saying, "Hi Shelly, this is David." The voice was nice and soothing and didn't startle me awake. I said hello aloud and there was lots of purple energy with my eyes closed and open. I thanked him for the communication. Now, I am wondering if David is a new guide or someone just stopping by to say Hi! I'm going to meditate in a bit to see if I get more information.
Yes, Davide (with an 'e' at the end) is a new guide. I didn't

hear him talking in my ear as I did before, but felt him. I used my pendulum and asked questions then wrote with him through automatic writing.

He said, "Hello dear one. The time is now for you to step forward and trust just as you tell everyone - trust all is happening as it should. You need to do this for yourself. Trust in the feelings and guidance you are receiving. All is unfolding in due time." Davide

March 28, 2012

I was awakened today at 6:08 am with a "Hi Honey" in a Heath Ledger Brokeback Mountain voice. I'm pretty sure this is not a guide!

An hour or so prior to that, I was awakened with a vision of a cityscape in purple. Energy rose from the city literally forming a heart. Once it was over the buildings, it burst into fireworks showering the city with LOVE. All of this was in purple energy and repeated several times. So cool!

April 2, 2012

I woke up this morning after having some really funky dreams last night. I wasn't scared, but they involved animals and people chasing me. I watched Frozen Planet on Discovery channel last night, so it could have played a role. The animals were alive and moving, but they were rotting and their fur had several oozy spots (sorry for the graphic depiction). I do not remember anything else.

April 3, 2012

I was awakened at 11:22 pm last night with half a phone ring. Nothing showed up on the caller id. I was unsure if it actually rang or if it was in my head, so I asked my husband if the phone just rang, which he verified for me. Throughout the night, I had numerous dreams. Most of the dreams involved a friend and taking care of children ranging in age from a baby to about ten years old.

April 5, 2012

I slept with the same set of crystals last night, but this time I actually grasped a tiger's eye, sodalite, and blue calcite in my right hand all night. Once again, I had lots of realistic dreams. I didn't recognize any of the locations, but some of the people were familiar.

After getting my daughter off to school, I opted to go back to bed. I haven't done this in a while, but felt the need to do so. I laid there for a while just listening to what I was hearing with the covers pulled over my head before finally falling asleep. Faces of people, mostly men, kept popping in. I distinctly remember two men with dark hair and eye glasses who were dressed in suits and very serious like they were at a funeral. I viewed them from above and at an angle rather that straight on. I didn't recognize either of them.

April 8, 2012

I laid in bed for quite some time last night before falling asleep. Heat was radiating from my body and every sound I heard was keeping me from falling asleep. I slept well and dreamed a lot, but cannot remember many details of the dreams other than I was traveling. I do distinctly remember being in a shuttle van and the driver handing me an envelope with my name on it. Inside of it was a $5,000 voucher for me to return.

April 9, 2012

Last night, my dreams involved schooling with several teachers in a variety of locations none of which I recognized. I distinctly remember taking a test and being up high on some sort of high-rise narrow bleachers trying to figure out how to make my way down.

April 10, 2012

I had nonsensical dreams last night for sure, and I remember them! We lived in a rectangular concrete house. It was drafty, so my mom and my stepdad thought we should move into a truck with a camper shell. I remember looking at them like they were nuts. Then, they were arguing about the high $80 water bill and opted to get a port-a-john (makes no sense to me) to cut costs.

My mom had a brilliant blue Cadillac with dings all over it. I didn't recognize the location and there wasn't anyone else in my dream. My mom looked like she did when I was first born with long hair. I didn't actually see my stepdad's face, but I assumed it was him. My room was small and cluttered with lots of stuff in it.

I'm going to begin week three coursework today starting with reading the material then moving into the daily exercises and meditations. I listened to the relaxation meditation first and the name Reginald immediately popped into my mind. Then, I listened to the meeting your Spirit guide meditation. I saw an image of a kind smiling black man dressed in white and holding a book.

I rested for an hour and received confirmation that several guides left with new ones coming in. I used the pendulum to validate the information that I was getting. I knew that I still had a guide who I was yet to connect with. I immediately got the name Cassie and an image of a strong female with long white hair and luminous skin. Her blue eyes are wide set and dominate her face. I see her as Light and see her hands, arms, shoulders, and face, but nothing else. She gestures with her hands and has the cupped-hand pageant wave down pat.

April 11, 2012

The first dream I had last night was a group of people gathered at a retreat. I recognized one woman, but none of the other people that were there or the location. People were paired off working together. The second dream was a banquet-type event with a lot of people. I recognized a co-worker from fourteen years ago. We were standing at a podium checking people in. I distinctly remember discussing with her an appropriate location to place the podium in order to catch everyone.

I listened to the relaxation meditation and then the meeting your Spirit guide meditation. I asked Raul to come forward, so that I could chat with him more. He looks like a cross between the singers Ricky Martin, singer/actor Desi Arnez and actor Ricardo

Montalban from Fantasy Island. He's dressed in a white suit.

I'm feeling a heaviness on my left side and in my left ear. I thanked him for his time.

I then asked to speak with Prof. Jedidiah Marshall. He's wearing a tweed jacket with patches on his elbow. He's got white hair and a white mustache. He looks like the actor Hal Holbrook. I see him sitting in a chair with his knees apart. I see him as a professor at a college in England and myself as a student of his (assuming this is a past life). I am wearing a dress with a coat over it, and my long brown hair is in a bun with a scarf over it. He was not a conventional teacher, and I wasn't a conventional student. I thanked him for his time and he waved without getting out of his chair.

April 12, 2012

Last night's dreams were extremely vivid, yet still didn't make sense to me. I visited my teenage home or a version of it. My mom, stepdad, brothers, stepsister, and stepbrothers were all there. I was awakened early in the morning with someone mowing the yard, and he wasn't mowing it right. I told my parents, and the guy stopped what he was doing. Then, I opened a cabinet door and a swarm of bees flew out. There were a lot of details in the dream. I am recognizing that Spirit is assisting me in paying attention to the details and to simply observe them rather than make sense of them.

I listened to the meeting your Spirit guide meditation. I asked Reginald to come forward, so that I could chat with him more. He is sitting on a step with his legs outstretched and is wearing brown pants and a white choir-type robe. He motions me to come sit by him.

I began typing the words I heard in my head:

Are you my only Spirit guide?
He smiles and laughs because I already know the answer.
How many do I have?
Seven at this time
Am I on the right spiritual path?

Of course my child, as you tell everyone else… you are exactly where you are supposed to be in this moment and in every moment.

Will you guide me to the next part of my Spirit journey?

Yes. I am one with you. I am here to offer you presence and peace of mind; hence my name – the peacekeeper. Allow yourself to be honored. Respect your time and energy.

I thanked Reginald for his time. He greeted me with clasped hands and a bowed head while nodding and saying "Namaste."

I then asked to connect with Cassie. Once again, I see only her upper body; yet no torso, just hands, arms, shoulders, and head. She is very beautiful and luminous. She appears to be floating in the air. I asked her about her role. She tells me that I did not have a true gatekeeper prior to her, but that it is imperative that I have one now. She assures me that she is efficient and organized just like me. I thanked Cassie for her time, and she raised her hand in a high-five sign and tossed her head around.

April 13, 2012

Once again, I had some AMAZING dreams last night. They were vivid and covered a lot of scenarios this time. One of them was that I was President Obama's daughter, and he was driving me to a small rural school. There was no secret service. It was just him and I in the black Cadillac SUV chatting away while he was taking me to school.

Then, I was at home where I am now doing yard work. A man in a powder blue older truck came to help me do the work. He looked like a friend of mine. We chatted and got started on the yard. In another dream, I was a student at a large school, but there weren't many other students there. I continually needed to leave class to go to the restroom or get something out of my locker.

April 15, 2012

I had a dream last night that I visited some friends in a city that I'm not familiar with. They lived in an unusual townhome-type residence. In order to gain access to their living quarters, you had to pull your body up through an access hole in the ceiling. It wasn't very big either. I distinctly remember analyzing and wondering how they carry their groceries inside. Looking down, a narrow staircase appeared.

I then left with my friend and began walking up the street to visit some places she wanted to show me. We passed by a grassy park-like area that had an assortment of blue pottery angels. All of the angels were broken and scattered with pieces lying everywhere. The artist/owner was upset, but had paintings of the angels intact. We had to climb over a fence to leave that area.

April 16, 2012

After getting ready for bed and when everyone else was asleep, I was guided to sit in the dark and call upon each of my guides one-by-one, asking them to come forward, so that I could feel their presence. I then asked them to show me what unconditional love feels like. It was a very powerful time.

April 18, 2012

I had an abundance of dreams last night and didn't recognize anyone or any place I visited. I was on a double-decker bus with a lot of people visiting a lot of places. The bus would drive into and through buildings. I visited a home that seemed to have many rooms with many inhabitants. As I walked through one door into another room, the scenery and people would be different, but I never walked outside.

April 19, 2012

OMG! What a night for sure! I had a series of dreams prior to being awakened at 1:13 am. They were at my husband's childhood home, and I was doing his laundry. The washer and dryer were outside in the grass. He wasn't there and his clothes were the size of a child rather than man-size. His mother and sister were not there, but his father who passed in 1994 was there passing through the house. We didn't speak, but he looked over his shoulder and smiled at me.

I tried to fall back to sleep, but tossed and turned for a couple of hours. This is where the excitement begins. I'm not sure if I was sleeping and dreaming or having visions. Many were cartoonish. I remember distinctly hearing the Bruno Mars song, "Just the Way You Are" playing in my right ear. This song also happens to be the ringtone on my phone. The lyrics, "…you are amazing just the way you are" kept repeating over and over again.

I remember seeing clear plastic tubing extending from my solar plexus to the left of me while I was lying down in bed. I started to show my husband the tubing when I saw a large hand above me reach for my hand and take it. I shuddered and tried to speak and realized that my husband was sleeping, I must have been dreaming and my hands were under the covers. I began having more visions, but do not remember what they were.

April 22, 2012

I remember having a lot of dreams and most occurred at the same place. A group of people were gathered together for a class. The housing seemed like a commune as it was definitely not a hotel. I didn't recognize anyone or the location. One of the teachers gave me a pendant that was an unfamiliar metallic crystal wrapped in wire. I also remember traveling on a transportation system that was nothing I had seen or heard of before. It was not a subway or tram, but rather smaller pods or boxes that would leave one location and appear in another. The last thing I remember is being at a place that was offering a buffet of assorted Mexican food. Lots of people were sitting at cafeteria-style tables. They were taking turns with three people at a time leaving their designated seat to fill their plates.

April 23, 2012

I remember having an abundance of dreams. My husband's alarm went off at 4:30 am. He woke me up to tell me that I was *talking in my sleep during the night. He said I was speaking gibberish and talking very quietly. He said I sounded sad and was sobbing.*

I do not remember that in my dream, but I do remember riding in his truck with him to a location because he wanted me to go with him. I was confused and then tried to figure out how I was going to get back home. He drove to a woman's house with my younger brother, who works for him. They were creating unusual "beds" for this woman, and I didn't like her energy. They were making grids and then putting assorted crystals within each grid square. My husband is a concrete finisher and pours concrete for residential house slabs and outsides, so none of this made any sense to me. There were other people there, and I remember feeling scared and threatened.

I also remember being in a car and someone was selling slushy kits for $5 each. They were literally Ziploc bags of crushed ice with assorted packets of flavoring. This confused me because I was rationalizing the cost.

∞

As you can see, I took this course very seriously and also had some pretty funky dreams. I felt like I was back in college again when I was doing the homework exercises as this was a certified course. The dates for the weekend workshop with Lisa Williams in Calabasas finally arrived, and I flew in on Thursday afternoon to connect with my friends. We enjoyed dinner and used the time to catch up. Forty-two individuals were selected by Lisa to participate in this fantastic opportunity. Friday and Saturday focused on learning. Saturday night, Robin, Anthony, and I gathered in my room to meditate and set our intentions. Once again, our time together proved to be very powerful and was most definitely a bonding experience.

On Sunday, each attendee was required to read for two clients from the general public. In order to pass the course, we had to successfully complete our homework and read for two people who would assess us. I was not nervous at all that morning. I went to my hotel room and meditated prior to each reading giving my client everything that I received. I felt very good afterwards acknowledging that I made connections with their loved ones in Spirit. Lisa's support in each one of us instilled within me the confidence that I had been seeking to truly be comfortable as a medium.

On my drive home from the airport the following Monday night, I reflected on what had transpired the past few years. As stated earlier, I had not heard of Lisa Williams prior to February 2010. She is authentic, real and human just like the rest of us. Lisa reiterated throughout the weekend, "I believe in you. I want you to succeed."

In addition to learning from Lisa, the time I spent with my friends that weekend reminded me that we are truly reflections of one another. "The stuff" we need to work on is reflected back to us as well as qualities we find endearing. The emotions and behaviors we experience are mirrored back to us. Yes, this means "the good, the bad, and the ugly." Not only did we learn from Lisa, but we learned from each other. We chose to be open and honest about our experiences and feelings as the weekend progressed. I believe this vulnerability was a catalyst for the shift that occurred and is still occurring within each one of us.

∞

Let the world know you as you are, not as you think you should be, because sooner or later, if you are posing, you will forget the pose, and then where are you? ~ Fanny Brice

Now able to fully acknowledge I am an Intuitive Medium, I realize that my beliefs will resonate with some individuals, but, more than likely, they will not resonate with everyone I know. I've discovered that it is essential to honor and respect my own beliefs as well as others' beliefs; that it is important to identify your beliefs, but it is equally important to acknowledge that not everyone has the same belief system as you.

This concept was reiterated to me when I opted to share some exciting news with my mom. Having completed Advanced Mediumship training with Lisa Williams, I received a personal telephone call from Lisa on May 15, 2012 notifying me that I had passed her course. Lisa told me that she loved my energy and how I worked with clients. She suggested that I focus my attention on developing one area and focus on going in one direction; otherwise, I could spread myself too thin. She told me that my gift is going to get stronger and stronger once I have totally surrendered to Spirit. Lisa picked up on my self-confidence issues as well.

I immediately called my friends as well as my dad and grandmother to share this news with them. I was then guided to contact my mom. I should mention that I had never actually discussed the work I do with her. I respect her religious beliefs and chose to not "go there" with her prior to the conversation I'm about to share with you. She knew that I practiced Reiki and didn't agree with the energy modality. How could I tell her that I also did intuitive readings and that I am a medium? To be honest, I felt at times as though I was keeping a secret from her — a very large one at that.

Nevertheless, I called her and shared with her my news. She listened, paused, exhaled deeply and said, "Shelly, I love you." She then went on to share her religious beliefs with me. I listened to her, acknowledged what she said, told her I loved her too, that I just wanted to share my happy news with her, and we ended the conversation. With that said, I do feel better because I am no longer keeping secrets from her, yet I understand that I should not discuss these matters with her again. In doing so, I am honoring and respecting her beliefs rather than blatantly being in-her-face with them. I choose to come from a place of love instead of invoking fear. I am proud of who I am and who I am becoming. I am shining my Light for all to see, or not see – as it is their choice.

With that being said, I must also share that when I received a friend request from my mom on Facebook, I waited a full thirty minutes before confirming the request. My mind immediately went to that "Oh no" place—as in, "Oh no! She is going to be able to see everything that I post as my status. What is she going to think now?" I confidently accepted the request as I acknowledged that they are her issues to deal with if she has any, and hopefully, she will develop a better understanding of the work I now do with Spirit.

∞

Life is life, and death is life, and everything in between.
~ Terri Guillemets

Since originally writing a draft of this book, Robin, Anthony and I studied platform mediumship with Lisa Williams in Calabasas, California in October 2012. The weekend was a reunion as many participants had also taken the advanced class in the spring. Providing me an opportunity to step out of my comfort zone and onto the stage, this workshop assisted me in delivering messages to an audience in a group setting.

After the class, I gathered up the energized self-confidence about my work, and began booking group readings and gallery events. The collective energy of those in attendance at such events tends to influence the evening and many times, there seems to be an underlying theme.

Deemed a time of connecting, receiving answers and healing, I can see and feel the shifts in energy occurring. Spirit utilizes these group settings as an opportunity to convey a message to many people at once—whether they are messages from their angels, guides or loved ones who have passed.

∞

Anthony and I also attended John Holland's Advanced Mediumship Master class in York, Maine on May 3-5, 2013. The scenic location of the workshop added to the ambiance of the weekend. We had views of the ocean, and John encouraged us to spend time outdoors during our breaks to ground our energy.

John's encouraging and gentle, but firm teaching style provided me the confidence to recognize that we are each unique, and it's okay to be that way. As he states, "the medium is the tube," and we should simply deliver the message. Drawing two diagonal lines on the sketch paper, he illustrates the information coming through the Crown Chakra and out our mouth. Referencing Psychic Medium John Edwards, he said "Deliver the mail. Don't read it."

Offering us plenty of opportunities to provide messages one-on-one and in a group setting, he made it very clear that there is no need to compare our style and technique to another person. My intention for taking the class was to provide more evidential information, including names, to my clients. Reading *People* magazine, I have the ability to remember celebrities and Spirit utilizes this knowledge to assist me in providing descriptions as well as names. In other words, Spirit uses what we have stored in our data bank—our brain—to convey the messages in a way that the client will understand.

• 18 •
I am a Reflection of You

With some people solitariness is an escape not from others but from themselves. For they see in the eyes of others only a reflection of themselves. ~ Eric Hoffer

**The characteristics you see in me; I see in you as well.
We are reflections of one another.**

HAVE YOU EVER ASKED THE question, "Who am I really?" Speaking for myself, I know that I am a woman, a wife, a mother, a daughter, a sister, a friend — but who am I really? I am all of these and also none of these. The truth of who I really am is that I am a soul in a physical body having a human experience because my soul chose to be incarnated on Earth at this time.

I could go on to describe my physical body with height, weight, eye color and hair color, but these are simply descriptions that will identify my body. My likes and dislikes just happen to be my personal preferences. I am a soul having physical, emotional, and mental experiences. The experiences I have had are just experiences. They do not define me nor will I allow them to. The memories of these experiences comprise the totality of my life as of this moment. As I continue to live my life, more of these experiences will encapsulate and become a part of my life, yet will not define me. I am at the center of my consciousness. I am aware that my perception - through my thoughts, emotions and senses — creates who I am.

Allow yourself to also embrace this clarity and greater knowing of who you really are. The knowledge you receive will help you to understand who you are, who you have been and who you are becoming.

∞

LIVING AUTHENTICALLY

A good character is the best tombstone. Those who loved you and were helped by you will remember you when forget-me-nots have withered. Carve your name on hearts, not on marble.
~ Charles H. Spurgeon

This beautiful quote by Charles H. Spurgeon has a much deeper meaning than simply reading the words at face value. The message for me is to be your authentic self always and in all ways, and individuals will remember you for that. Some people go through life allowing others to only see what they choose to present rather than being their true selves all of the time. So many adjectives may describe what a good character is — integrity, honesty, authenticity, truthfulness, virtue, kindness, regard for others...

Living authentically involves being genuine with all people you come into contact with all of the time.

During a reincarnation class in July 2011, Steffany Barton guided the attendees in a group past-life regression. The term, reincarnation, is the belief shared by many of the world's religions that we are born again after we die—meaning our soul continues to live after our physical body ceases to exist. I received clarity on my current experiences, and I acknowledge they involved a past life.

During the thirty minute past life regression meditation, I noted the following experiences:

> I felt a washing all over my body. I heard crinkling in my left ear like wind blowing. I saw a beach and palm trees and then SWOOSH...I was somewhere else. It definitely wasn't Egypt. I saw and felt sand on my toes and feet. There was a stone walkway below and above me with spaces left open for windows. I was dressed in a long red satin or silk gown. I found an ornate mirror to view myself, and I was wearing a headdress. I'm sitting on a tall stone chair, which I do not believe to be a throne. However, disciples are bowing down to me. I see a dark gargoyle costumed figure creeping and crouching down. He was very scary looking.

The pivotal moment that I saw was when a figure came up behind me with a long ax and split me into two halves. I saw a white entity composed of light (not necessarily a bird, maybe my soul) leave my body and move upwards.

The following is Steffany Barton's past life interpretation:

> On the past life regression, you were a Cardinal from the Catholic church, but also moonlighted as a pagan. You had an angel on one shoulder and a devil on the other, so to speak (you can decide which was the angel and which was the devil...the church or the cult). Anyway, the church got wind

of your secret life and killed you. Oops! You've got to be who you are with everyone.

∞

May this story be an example for you just as it is for me—do not be afraid to be yourself. There is no need to hide aspects of yourself; allow the real deal to shine through always. Be real - be your true self! Individuals will appreciate you for being YOU. Do not hide behind a false front.

When you align your thoughts, words and actions with your beliefs, you are living authentically. I assure you that it is liberating to do so! Believe in yourself, yet know that other people will not always see things your way. Honor and respect their beliefs, but stand in your power and be true to YOU! The time is now to start living your life the way you want to be remembered. Focus your energy on being the best you can be and living a life without regret, so that you can live fully.

∞

In February 2013, my dear friend Jackie posed some questions to me. As the facilitator of Sacred Circle Retreats, she asked me to go within to let my Spirit speak. The intent of Sacred Circle Retreats is to 1) create and facilitate virtual spiritual retreats, 2) birth a hub of soul connection, growth and healing, and 3) invoke a powerful circle of Divine energy. Together, we were exploring what would be suitable for me to offer as one of the guides.

1. What makes my heart sing?
Being acknowledged, valued, appreciated and loved as

well as doing the same for others. Allowing myself to see how we are all interwoven, yet having our own unique human life experience. I love doing the "work" that I do— watching the unfolding, the "ah-ha" moments, seeing myself in other people. I love empowering and encouraging others to make their own life choices without relying on others. I really love having authentic, comfortable conversations.

2. What are my true gifts?

Being ME - knowing what to say and when. I always seem to find the "right" words to convey or shall I say rather than finding, I listen and trust—whether I am speaking or writing. I know that someone needs to hear the message coming through at the time.

3. What are my areas of expertise that I could teach/share with others?

My life experiences—healing, having patience, developing my gifts, attaining confidence, empowerment, courage, releasing fear, overcoming self-perceived obstacles. As with all "good" teachers, they teach what they know. It's not necessarily something that we have studied; instead, it is what we have lived.

4. If I could do anything and get paid for my time, what would that anything be?

I really love speaking to groups of people—the interaction, seeing/feeling their energy shift, listening to the questions they ask, hearing their voice, offering encouragement. I love the one-on-one interaction when I do readings as well. I especially enjoy doing them in-person at the spirit fairs where I can look them in their eyes and really acknowledge their presence. Recognizing who I was just a few years ago, the idea of speaking in front of even a small group of people invoked a tremendous amount of fear and nervousness. I am amazed at how much I have "grown!"

∞

As spiritual beings having a human life experience, each one of us is derived from Source energy. Recognizing that we are each connected, our intentions should be to acknowledge that we are reflections of one another. Though our experiences and life circumstances may differ, ultimately we are all One.

I am You ~ You are Me ~ We are ONE

As Lightworkers, we are here to assist individuals on their spiritual journey, raise the vibration of humanity as a whole, and elevate global consciousness. Let us consciously choose to be ONE together. Let us see our reflection in another and acknowledge it.

I am a Reflection of YOU

• SECTION THREE •

Tools to Assist You
on Your Spiritual Journey

During my journey into consciousness, I have utilized many tools that assisted in my progression.

In this section, I share the tools and wisdom that helped me the most, those that I have found to be straightforward, uncomplicated, and therefore, easily incorporated into our daily lives.

• 19 •
Teaching What I Know

The best teachers teach from the heart, not from the book.
~ Author Unknown

**Through our life experiences, we are each gathering
wisdom and tools for our spiritual tool belt to assist us,
as well as others, on this journey.**

THE BEST KIND OF TEACHER teaches what they
know. Simply speaking, you would not want a math
teacher to teach English or an English teacher to teach
math. There are a multitude of modalities, books, and
teachers when it comes to the many facets of spirituality.
Typically, you will learn the most when you feel a
connection to your teacher or if the material or book
resonates with you. Practicing discernment and
acknowledging what feels right to you is essential. If
something does not resonate with you, please practice
discernment and choose not to accept it for yourself. In

other words, accept what resonates and discard the rest. Do not feel like it has to be all or nothing. I have had many lessons in discernment. Trust me; I didn't always learn the lesson the first time around. It took numerous attempts for me to really have an understanding of this concept and to feel comfortable honoring what resonates with my be-ing.

A teacher's purpose is not to create students in his own image,
but to develop students who can create their own image.
~ Author Unknown

I acknowledge that many teachers and authors have walked this path and have had similar experiences as I have. I know that much of this information is probably not new to you. However, I am offering you my perception and interpretation of what has assisted me on my own journey. I am guided to include this wisdom for you to read, review, and because you have free will, to accept what feels right to you.

These tools run the gamut of basic information that bears repeating to wisdom that is easily incorporated into one's daily life. I invite you to incorporate these tools and implement them as you are guided to do so. Remember, spirituality is a way of life rather than simply a practice. The recommendations noted in this chapter are not listed in any degree of importance, and this information has also been presented in *28 Days to a New YOU* and *Connect to the YOU Within*. It bears repeating here:

Assess Relationships

Clearing the energetic clutter, so to speak, within relationships is sometimes necessary. Take a moment to reflect and assess those relationships that you perceive to be healthy and balanced while also acknowledging those relationships that you may deem unhealthy or imbalanced. Making the conscious decision to cultivate the healthy relationships as well as establish boundaries within those relationships that are perceived to be unhealthy and imbalanced is essential for your personal well-being. As you grow spiritually and change, your relationships with others will change as well. There is no need to evaluate the particulars of this change as it is inevitable.

Remember, the Law of Attraction assists in bringing new people into your life as previous relationships come to a close. As far as family members go, you may choose to spend more time with some family members and less time with others.

Avoid Miscommunication

Present day communication surpasses just face-to-face contact. We can Skype, chat, talk on the phone, email, and text. The advances made in technology are nothing short of extraordinary. Effective communication involves communicating clearly, whether you are the sender or the receiver of the message.

Clearly speaking or conveying the message via written means is only part of communicating clearly. The other part involves being clear about what you are expressing. Be sure to say what you really mean, thus avoiding any doubt for the listener or reader. Be clear when expressing what you mean. Sometimes, you have to spell-it-out rather than be vague. Having to "read between the lines" inhibits effective communication – both for the sender and the receiver.

Remember, communication involves both listening and speaking. Pay attention to the verbal and nonverbal feedback you are receiving during communication whether it is in-person, over the phone or via written word. Being an effective listener may require you to relay back to the sender what you have heard and interpreted in order to make sure that you have heard the message correctly.

Be Mindful of Word Choices

What you focus on becomes your reality with the Law of Attraction; therefore, it is very important to pay attention to your thoughts, words, and actions. Be mindful of the energy you are putting out there.

Listen to the words you utter daily. Express what you desire rather than your present state of be-ing. Be clear about what you mean. Avoid using the words trying or hoping when declaring what you want as it evokes doubt. Leave it out of the sentence completely. Use the words "I am" whenever possible as it is a declaration of what you desire.

I encourage you to practice being cognizant of your thoughts, words and actions. This really does take time and effort. You may choose to practice by typing or writing the words you are speaking. Look at what you have typed or written. Can you say the same thing in another, more positive, life-affirming way? More than likely, you can! Becoming aware of the words you are using takes time and lots of practice. Listening to other individuals is much easier. I suggest that you really listen when others are speaking and pay attention to their word choices. It will assist you in becoming more aware of your own vocabulary.

Be Present

It is time to let go of the past, live in the present, and look to the future—for it is this attitude that will transform you. The past is in the past; it cannot be changed. Only your perception of the experiences can change. It is nice to look to the future, but you don't want to miss out on the present in doing so.

Your mind, body, and spirit should be unified in one specific physical place right now in order to be fully present. Being present involves living in the moment rather than focusing on the future or dwelling in the past. Focus on living, be-ing and breathing in the moment.

Focus your energy on being present and in the NOW at this very moment. Be observant and become aware of your surroundings, yet allow yourself to simply BE. What do you see? What do you hear? What do you feel? What do you know? Allow yourself to become fully aware and completely present right here, right now. Do not allow your mind to wander. Become cognizant of this moment. Breathe in deeply and exhale mindfully. Feel your chest expanding as you breathe in and your chest deflating as you exhale. Feel your heart beating rhythmically as blood is coursing through your veins. All you should feel at this moment is being present. Continue being mindful of your breathing and relax. You are present in this moment.

Breathe

Take a moment to breathe in deeply and exhale anyone and anything that no longer serves you. Be mindful of your inhalations and your exhalations. Two to three times a day for 2-3 minutes, I invite you to clear your mind and open your heart. Visualize yourself breathing in emerald green energy from Archangel Raphael and exhaling the pain, hurt, fear, frustration, worry and doubt. Release it and let it go.

Celebrate You

Your birthday is your special day! Your birthday is the day in which your family and friends celebrate you and your entry into the earth plane. Why limit this celebration to one day a year? Celebrate YOU and all that you are each and every day.

Rejoice in All That Is! I see that you are an amazing individual. See yourself as an amazing individual as well. Say aloud and say it proud, "I AM AMAZING!" Allow yourself to really feel how amazing you are. Celebrate all that you are and all that you are becoming.

You are making a difference in the lives of others by simply being YOU. No extra work is required. By setting an example and shining your Light bright, you allow others to do the same. Do not doubt the power that you hold within.

Center Your Energy

As energetic beings, it is important to ground, center and protect your energy.

Centering involves finding that calm spot deep inside yourself that is eternal being-ness. I like to visualize a white ball of light at my core in the stomach area. Take a few deep breaths and bring awareness inward to the central essence - that place that is peaceful and serene no matter what the external circumstance.

Remember to ground, protect, and center your energy daily. We are all of the same energy, but we are each having our own human life experiences

Clear and Balance Chakras

Clearing and balancing your chakras (energy centers) is an easy task to accomplish. Doing so clears the energetic clutter, so to speak, and revitalizes your energy. As you become more adept at visualizing the chakras and their associated colors, you can do this very quickly. You may even choose to do this in the shower just as I do. As the water cleanses my physical body, I am clearing and balancing my energetic body. *Note: A chakra clearing and balancing exercise is included in Chapter 20.*

Cut Cords

Every person you have had a relationship or even simply an encounter with, you have a "cord" between you. This is an energetic cord. It's healthy to cut these cords periodically saying, "I cut cords to anyone and anything that no longer serves me or my Higher purpose" while either doing a cutting or chopping motion in front of your solar plexus/belly button area. The cords you are cutting are lower vibration cords associated with fear, worry, doubt, guilt, shame, frustration, regret, etc. Cords associated with love will "grow" back instantaneously, so there is no reason to fear cutting cords.

Express your Gratitude

Gratitude is an expression of thankfulness. The simple words, "thank you," extend far beyond their utterance. They are an acknowledgement of appreciation. Thanking another individual for having completed a task, the extension of a hand in friendship, and even the recognition of a compliment will reflect the gratitude you are feeling. In addition, acknowledging and expressing gratitude for all you are thankful for assists you in becoming a better YOU. In doing so, we remind ourselves of what we do have rather than focusing solely on our desires.

I believe that the more we emit gratitude energy out into the Universe and the more that we open ourselves to being in the flow - the more we will be amazed at the outcome.

Express Yourself

Do a mini life review and assess how you feel. Take a moment to write down what you "like" and what you "do not like" about your life as it is now. Take a moment to write down your desires, your dreams, your aspirations and intentions on a piece of paper. You are worthy to receive and to achieve all that you desire. A thought becomes tangible once it is written on paper. It takes form. You can see the words and touch the paper. Read what you have written and see how you feel when reading it.

Express your desires and intentions creatively. Creating a vision or dream board is a wonderful way to turn thoughts into words and pictures. You can flip through old magazines and cut out pictures or even search images on the Internet and print them off. Include any words, phrases, and quotes that resonate with you. Do not hesitate to think BIG either. The images you have chosen reflect your dreams, so dream big!

Your imagination is truly the limit; otherwise, you have no boundaries. Glue or tape the images to cardboard or poster board and hang them in a location that you will see throughout the day. Feel free to add or remove words and images whenever you are guided to as well. This is your creation!

Forgive Yourself

Forgive yourself just as you would forgive another individual. Do not admonish yourself for the previous decisions you made and now regret. Every choice you made was absolutely the right choice at the time you made it with the information you had available to you at the time.

Learning from our experiences and not repeating them is a benefit to having them to begin with. Do not allow those experiences to define you. Release yourself from the pain, heartache, and frustration you have been holding on to. The past is in the past. It cannot be changed. Allow yourself to let go, so that you can begin anew! New beginnings start with the release of old thoughts. Choose to believe there are no mistakes—only opportunities for learning and growth.

Ground Your Energy

As energetic beings, it is important to ground, center and protect your energy. Grounding your energy keeps you present and in the moment. It completes the energy circuit and anchors your energy to the earth below. Keeping firmly planted energetically helps prevent feelings of fuzziness or spacey-ness that can often disperse your personal energy.

Visualize energy passing from the Root Chakra to the

center of the Earth, or tree roots sprouting from the bottom of the feet. Going barefoot indoors, gently stomping your feet a few times, and walking outside in the grass or on the pavement are ways to ground your energy as well. Crystals such as hematite, tourmaline, and smoky quartz work well, too. Not only do these crystals assist in grounding and protecting one's energy, but they also dissolve negativity and harmonize mind, body, and spirit.

You can also ground your energy by visualizing the Earth having a huge white heart of light in the center of it. Visualize an anchor of white light coming from your heart to the Earth's heart grounding you in love and Light.

Honor your Beliefs

Identifying and honoring your personal beliefs is necessary, but it is equally important to acknowledge that not everyone has the same belief system as you. Having the courage to express your beliefs to others and not being afraid of what they might think involves fortitude. Allowing yourself to be who you really are with all people requires that you stand in your power. Standing in your power simply means "owning" what you believe to be true. Emanating this power in your words and actions requires no effort or thought when you allow yourself to just BE. It definitely does take courage to be your authentic self.

Increase Awareness

Awareness involves both consciousness and cognizance. This includes being cognizant of our surroundings and the people coming into and leaving our life. The Universe will assist us in bringing people, teachers and experiences into our awareness, so that we can learn, heal, and grow.

Increase your awareness level by focusing and tuning in with each of your five senses. Spend time each day being cognizant of your surroundings. What do you hear? What do you see? What do you taste? What do you smell? What do you feel? Make notes in your journal of your experiences as you are guided to do so.

As you become accustomed to paying attention, it will be easier to notice when you are not distracted. Silence your mind chatter and sit in quiet repose. Take note of the guidance you are receiving and the signs you are observing. Remember that these signs may be in the form of cloud formations; nature, such as birds or butterflies; songs on the radio; overhead conversations, etc. Do not second-guess if you are actually receiving a sign even though you may not understand the meaning of the sign at the moment you receive it. Simply acknowledge it, express your gratitude for it and you will understand the meaning of the sign when you are supposed to.

Journal Daily

Journaling daily is recommended as it will assist you in recognizing who you were, who you are, and who you are becoming. Write down your thoughts, feelings, and emotions as you are guided to throughout the day. Pay attention to bodily sensations as well. Read back through what you have written whenever you are guided to.

Keep in mind that there is no right way or wrong way to journal—only your way. You may opt to keep a handwritten notebook or maintain a document on your computer or even both as I do. Do not constrain your expression by feeling obligated to write for a specific amount of time. Simply allow the words to flow. For many individuals, their blog is their journal. I can attest that journaling assisted me greatly with my awakening and opening up to Spirit. Plus, it really helped me to remember my dreams.

Live Authentically

Living authentically involves striving to be genuine

with all people you come into contact with all of the time. Do not be afraid to be yourself. There's no need to hide aspects of yourself; allow the "real deal" to shine through always. When you align your thoughts, words and actions with your beliefs, you are living authentically. I assure you that it is liberating to do so. Believe in yourself, yet know that other people will not always see things your way. Honor and respect their beliefs, but stand in your power and be true to YOU!

The time is now to start living your life the way you want to be remembered. Focus your energy on being the best you can be and living a life without regret, so that you can live fully.

Love Yourself

Focus on loving yourself. Doing so isn't selfish; it is self-love. Be especially mindful of your self-talk. You are worthy to receive the same love that you give out. Don't doubt your ability to love and to be loved. See yourself as the Divine sees you — a beautiful, unique and miraculous creation. There is no one else like you nor will there ever be. When you really love yourself and open your heart to love, you will attract this same love back into your life from another.

Practice expressing verbally love for YOU. Look in a mirror and tell yourself, "I love you." You can do this in the morning when you are brushing your teeth and combing your hair. It is important for you to mean it. Allow yourself to truly feel the love you have inside of yourself. This exercise will make you smile; it may even make you laugh — especially with your first attempt. Laughter is healing. You may feel emotional as well. Allow yourself to feel what you are feeling. There is no shame in crying when doing this exercise, and tears are cleansing. Cross your arms and wrap them around you, giving yourself a hug! Breathe in deeply and exhale. All is well.

Meditate

Take time each day to connect with YOU, your inner self, through meditation. The act of meditation takes many forms. It can be sitting quietly in reflection, listening to a guided meditation, going for a walk or spending time outdoors in nature. For some individuals, reading is a form of meditation. The intent of meditation is to just BE and listen.

Allowing yourself to listen to the guidance you are receiving and to be present in this moment assists you in your transformation.

Perhaps, you may even be guided, just as I am, to pause from what you are doing periodically throughout the day, close your eyes, sit silently for a few minutes to connect, and then resume the activity. Throughout the day and even now as I am writing, I will do exactly that. I stop when I am guided to. Although it may be just for a few minutes, those minutes have an extremely powerful effect. Not only do I feel refreshed and energized, but my concentration is typically enhanced, and I am able to accomplish more in less time. *Note: Chapter 21 offers several guided meditations. You may choose to record the words, so that you can listen to them.*

Mind, Body, Spirit as ONE

We are more than a physical body. We must recognize that we are a spiritual being in a physical body having a human life experience. It is important to cultivate the spirit, yet equally important to honor the mind and body. Therefore, I ask you to acknowledge that the mind, body, and spirit are ONE—a unified entity. Balancing the aspects of mind, body, and spirit is an integral part of each individual's overall well-being.

A healthy diet along with exercise is necessary for your physical well-being. Be mindful of your dietary intake as food has an energetic vibration. Fresh fruits and vegetables assist in raising your vibration; whereas processed or fast foods have a lower vibration and may leave you feeling lethargic. In order to be healthy, we must feel healthy. Notice how your body reacts and how you feel after eating certain foods. Eating in moderation is essential. Over-indulgence only leads to a tummy ache later. Take note of how your body feels after consuming certain foods. Walking is not a strenuous exercise, yet it does get the "heart pumping" and the blood circulating if you walk at a brisk pace.

Mental exercises, such as memory games, Sudoku, crossword and word seek puzzles, stimulate your brain. Assessing relationships and choosing to allow some relationships to "run their course," so to speak, is necessary for your mental health. As you make the conscious effort to maintain healthy relationships and end unhealthy ones, you are taking control of your life. In doing so, you are contributing to your mental health.

Your physical, mental, emotional and spiritual health are equally important and should be acknowledged accordingly.

Non-Attachment to the Outcome

I encourage you to practice non-attachment to the outcome of a particular experience, especially when there is more than one person involved. Each individual will have their own perception of the experience. It is next to impossible to alter someone's perception. In circumstances that you don't see "eye-to-eye" with another, simply listen and then practice non-attachment to the end results (observe, allow, let go). This means that you are recognizing what you have heard, but you are not allowing another individual's perception to influence your own.

In addition, be sure to have the courage to ask the question(s) you want to ask in regards to any experience, but remember to release attachment to the outcome. In other words, make your wishes known, but release the time constriction of its occurrence or the possibility of it happening at all. Sometimes the answer will be—yes, no, maybe, or not now. And remember, you cannot dictate what is beyond your control.

Pay Attention

Pay attention to the guidance you are receiving from your Higher Self, your angels and your guides. Sometimes, this guidance is subtle and comes in whispers and gentle nudges. When we refuse to acknowledge this guidance, it becomes louder, more persistent and may feel like the proverbial push or shove. It is important to recognize and acknowledge the guidance you are receiving and give thanks for it. You may not understand the how, when, why, what or where aspects of the guidance, yet you should acknowledge it and express gratitude for receiving it.

Pay attention to the messages your body is sending you. Listen to your gut instinct, which is located in your Solar Plexus Chakra. As you become attuned to listening to your body and what it is telling you, it will become easier to recognize the messages that originate from this area. Your physical body is a great device for gauging energy and situations. If something does not feel right, do not proceed. The guidance may be a subtle whisper or a gentle nudge. Other times, the guidance may become louder and more persistent.

Recognizing and acknowledging the guidance you are receiving assists you in becoming more aware—more "in tune" with you. Also, pay attention to what I refer to as "chills" or buzzing. Whenever this occurs, I immediately verbally acknowledge these sensations because I recognize them to be validation from Spirit that what I am saying is correct. It is Spirit's way of saying, "You are on to something."

As you are guided to throughout the day, find a quiet

peaceful place where you can practice listening to the guidance you are receiving. It will be easier to hear when you are not distracted by outside noise. You may choose to meditate briefly or simply be present and listen.

Practice Kindness

Smiling, offering a kind word to another and holding the door open are effortless acts that have meaningful results. Both the recipient and the giver walk away from the interaction affected in some way. No gesture is too small nor goes unnoticed.

These simple acts will not only raise the recipient's vibration, but will raise your vibration as the giver or sender as well. Practice compassion with everyone you come into contact with, including passersby in the store. It is really easy to do and both individuals will feel lighter and shine their own Lights brighter. In turn, you will attract individuals into your life who are a reflection of you. Realize that you are making a difference in the lives of others by being who you really are.

Protect Your Energy

As energetic beings, it is important to ground, center and protect your energy.

Protecting, also known as shielding, is important to keep yourself protected from another's "junk" and helps keep personal energy separated. Visualizing a white light or a bubble surrounding you will help protect and shield you. Some people prefer to envision themselves wrapped in a cloak, wearing a cape or carrying a shield. Use what feels most comfortable and resonates best with your energy at the time. Only love can penetrate this protective shield — everything else will be dispelled and fall way.

Shift Your Perception

Perception is how we view or perceive an experience through our senses—sight, taste, touch, smell and sound. We may choose to label an experience as good or bad, positive or negative. In reality, this is simply our perception or a personal assessment of the experience. Changing your perception assists you in changing your life. Remove the constraints of the "box" you have created for yourself, and allow yourself to view experiences from another individual's point of view.

A group of people may have all had the exact same experience, but will each perceive the experience differently based on their own perspective. It is next to impossible to alter someone's perception.

In circumstances that you do not see "eye-to-eye," simply listen and then practice non-attachment to the outcome. This means that you are recognizing what you have heard, but you are not allowing another individual's perception to influence your own.

Shine Your Light Bright

The time is now for you to shine your Light bright! This Light is your Life Force—your spark. Each one of us has the Divine spark within us. It is our right to be all that we are intended to be and so much more. Do not allow anyone to dim your light under any circumstances. This is your life, and you are creating it with your thoughts, words, and actions. As a spiritual being, you have free will and the power to make choices. You are perfect and whole in every way. Shine your Light brightly for all to see!

As the song lyrics emphasize, "This little Light of mine, I'm gonna let it shine... let it shine, let it shine, let it shine..."

Spend Time in Reflection

Silence your mind chatter and sit in quiet

contemplation. Take a moment to perceive what your Light is and what shining your Light truly means to you. Spend time in reflection and appreciate the magnificent capacity you behold within you. Allow memories to gently surface into your conscious mind of when your Light had been dimmed by others as well as when you dimmed your Light yourself by choice. Allow powerful memories to fill your body, mind and soul of when you shined your Light bright. Take note of any feelings you experience as you do so.

Stand in Your Power

Allowing yourself to be who you really are with all people all of the time requires that you stand in your power. This involves communicating your needs and desires to others as well as to yourself. Standing in your power simply means "owning" what you believe to be true and then speaking your truth. Emanating this power in your words and actions requires no thought when you become accustomed to doing so.

Throughout your life, some people may try to control you or the choices you are making. When you allow this to happen, you are either consciously or subconsciously giving your power away to another. Do you recognize when this happens? How does it make you feel?

Any time a pattern or experience repeats itself, it is important to acknowledge it and then allow yourself to see things from a Higher perspective. These experiences will continue to repeat themselves until you recognize the lesson the experience is offering. You may ask, "What am I supposed to learn from this experience. Why do I feel this way?"

Take Time for You

Individuals need balance in their life. Having balance involves taking time for others and taking time for oneself. You may feel "stretched thin" if you do not have this balance. Notice how I have used the word take rather than make. There are twenty-four hours in a day. A new day begins when those hours are expended. We are unable to make the day longer; therefore, we cannot make time. We can only take time. Simply taking time does not have a monetary cost, yet it creates abundance in the form of happiness, health, and well-being.

Trust in the Process

Trusting in the process means to have confidence in the process and to have confidence in yourself. You are permitting yourself to do something without fear of the outcome. You are going full-steam ahead knowing that this is your life to live. You are living a life of purpose! Your purpose is to simply be YOU and to have the human life experiences you are intended to have.

Trust that everything is happening how and when it is supposed to. The Universe does not operate on human's linear time; it operates on Divine time. Fear and worry serve no purpose other than creating more fear and worry. They go hand and hand inhibiting and creating blockages in our life. Fear tends to suppress living because we avoid taking risks in life. We are fearful of the outcome or what others may think of us, so we avoid taking the risk altogether.

Growth takes time. Remember, a seed doesn't become a flower overnight! It takes watering, nurturing, and sunlight, which translates spiritually to taking time for you as well as basking in the love and light!

Some days, you may feel like you are taking a step backward or you may feel like you are having a "bad" day. Honor yourself and your feelings. This is part of the process.

As you continue to grow and evolve, you will have a greater understanding of seeing every experience as an opportunity for learning and growth. Although we humans function on linear time with clocks and calendars, the Universe operates on Divine time. This means that everything is happening exactly as it is supposed to in Divine time.

Use Positive Affirmations

The use of affirmations work in unison with the Law of Attraction. The energy that you project with your thoughts, words and actions is reflected back to you. Affirmations can be short, simple and to the point, or they can be longer and more detailed. The choice is yours.

I have provided you with a few of my favorite affirmations that I use:

Affirm ~ My heart overflows with gratitude and joy. I am conscious of being present in this moment. I recognize the guidance I am receiving. I am allowing myself to simply breathe. I acknowledge and appreciate that I am not alone for my angels and guides are with me always.

Affirm ~ My heart overflows with gratitude and joy. I am conscious of being present in this moment. I recognize that I am a creator, and I am creating my reality. I am allowing myself to simply breathe. I am surrendering to the Universe anything and anyone that no longer serves me or my Higher purpose. I am releasing it now fully and completely. I choose to create my life and all of its experiences consciously.

Affirm ~ I recognize that I am not the same person I was yesterday nor will I be the same person tomorrow that I am today. My spirit is continually healing and growing. I recognize my power as I tap into my inner knowingness. I trust in the process as it unfolds.

Affirm ~ My heart overflows with gratitude and joy. I am conscious of being present in this moment. I recognize that people may be in my life for a reason, a season or a lifetime. I am allowing myself to simply breathe. I acknowledge and appreciate that when a relationship may end, it is making room for a new relationship to begin.

Affirm ~ I honor the Light within me. I honor the Light within me. I honor the Light within me.

Affirm ~ My heart overflows with gratitude and joy. I am conscious of being present in this moment. I recognize that I am love and I am loved. I am allowing myself to simply breathe.

Work with Crystals

Crystals have powerful energetic properties. They can be used as psychic protection, to clear and balance chakras, as psychic tools, and for healing. Each crystal has its own specific healing attributes. Although I can identify many crystals and their healing properties, as I stated before, the mass of my crystal collection has been acquired by listening to the guidance I receive. Simply speaking, I know when a crystal needs to come home with me. *The Crystal Bible: A Definitive Guide to Crystals* by Judy Hall is an excellent resource to learn more about the crystal's properties and attributes.

• 20 •
Chakra Work

WHAT ARE CHAKRAS?

Chakras are energy-awareness centers.
They are the revolving doors of creativity and communication
between Spirit and the world. ~ Michael J. Tamura

Keep your chakras cleared and balanced.
As you clean your physical body,
clear your energetic body.

CHAKRAS ARE SPINNING WHEELS OF light that act as energy transformers. They take the Life Force that is all around us and transform it into the various frequencies we need, bringing them into our subtle energy system. Chakras are shaped like the circular motion of water flowing down a drain.

In addition to the major chakras, minor chakras are in

the hands, feet, knees and other parts of the body. Each chakra extends out from the spine with the front side generally involved with receiving subtle energy while the backside is generally involved with sending energy out, although it is possible for the direction to change back and forth from time to time.

∞

CHAKRAS EXPLAINED

1. The Root Chakra, also known as the Base Chakra, is red and is located at the bottom of the torso near the tip of the tailbone. The energy the Root Chakra supplies creates the will to live and is involved with our need for food, shelter, clothing and the basic necessities of life.

2. The Sacral Chakra is orange and is located just above the pubic bone. The Sacral Chakra supplies energy for sexuality, reproduction, the enjoyment of life, and the physical attraction in relationships. It is also one of the areas where guilt is hidden.

3. The Solar Plexus Chakra is yellow and is located just below the sternum, near the diaphragm. The Solar Plexus Chakra is involved with self-expression, taking action in the world, confidence and personal power. It can also be a place where fear and anger is held. This is your "gut instinct" and your power center.

4. The Heart Chakra is green and is located in the center of the chest. The Heart Chakra supplies energy for all aspects of love, joy, compassion and surrender. It supplies all parts of the energy field with nurturing and can be a source of spiritual connection and guidance.

5. The Throat Chakra is blue and is located in the throat area. It supplies energy for speaking, thinking, communicating, writing and creative expression. The

Throat Chakra can also be involved with clairaudience, contemplation and inner guidance. It is one pathway through which our feelings are expressed.

6.   The Third Eye Chakra is indigo or purple and is located between the eyebrows. The Third Eye Chakra supplies energy for self-awareness, higher consciousness, clairvoyance, inner vision, conceptual thinking, planning and insight. In meditation, the third eye is a pathway to higher dimensions and higher consciousness.

7.   The Crown Chakra is white and is located at the top of the head and points upward. The Crown Chakra's energy connects with the Spirit realms including higher consciousness and the Higher Power. It is one of the pathways to enlightenment.

∞

CLEARING AND BALANCING CHAKRA EXERCISE

This is a quick and effective exercise to assist you in clearing and balancing your chakras. Please know that you can do this exercise whenever you feel guided to. You may choose to do it daily as you take time for YOU!

Take a moment to just BE. Sit in a chair with your back straight and your palms up, open to receiving. Close your eyes. You may wish to visualize the chakras and their respective colors as fruits, vegetables or even flowers.

Begin with the Root Chakra ~ This is your area of survival needs and where the lower vibration energies of worry, fear, doubt, guilt, shame, regret and frustration reside. Visualize this chakra as red, beautiful, healthy, balanced and cleared. Breathe in deeply, green healing energy from Archangel Raphael and exhale anything and anyone that no longer serves you. Release the fear and worry.

Move up to the Sacral Chakra ~ This is your area of creativity and sexuality. Visualize this chakra as orange, beautiful, healthy, balanced and cleared. Breathe in deeply, green healing energy from Archangel Raphael and exhale anything and anyone that no longer serves you. Begin to create the life you desire by allowing yourself to be in the flow of manifestation.

Move up to the Solar Plexus Chakra ~ This is your gut instinct, your knowingness, your power center. Visualize this chakra as yellow, beautiful, healthy, balanced and cleared. Breathe in deeply, green healing energy from Archangel Raphael and exhale anything and anyone that no longer serves you. It is important for you to stand in your power and be true to you.

Move up to the Heart Chakra ~ This is the area where love resides. Visualize this chakra as green, beautiful, healthy, balanced and cleared. Allow your heart to open fully to receive the same love that you send out. Breathe in deeply, green healing energy from Archangel Raphael and exhale anything and anyone that no longer serves you. Allow this energy to fill your lungs and flow through your veins. Know that you are love and you are loved.

Move up to the Throat Chakra ~ This is your voice; your area of communication. Visualize this chakra as blue, beautiful, healthy, balanced and cleared. Breathe in deeply, green healing energy from Archangel Raphael and exhale anything and anyone that no longer serves you. Choose to communicate your needs and desires to yourself and to others. Speak your truth always and in all ways.

Move up to the Third Eye Chakra ~ This is your area of psychic awareness. Visualize this chakra as indigo, beautiful, healthy, balanced and cleared. Breathe in deeply, green healing energy from Archangel Raphael and exhale anything and anyone that no longer serves you. Connect to your intuition—the YOU within.

And lastly, you are at the Crown Chakra ~ This is your

connection to Source, The Higher Power, All That Is ~ Visualize this chakra as white, beautiful, healthy, balanced and cleared. Breathe in deeply, green healing energy from Archangel Raphael and exhale anything and anyone that no longer serves you.

Once again, breathe in deeply the healing energy; and exhale your pain, worry, fear, frustration, anger, regret, shame and anything and everything that no longer serves you. Release and let it go! Your chakras have been cleared and balanced. You are love and you are loved. And so it is!

∞

UTILIZING CRYSTALS FOR CHAKRA BALANCING

You may also be guided to work with crystals to clear and balance your chakras. You may choose to select crystals or allow them to select you; then work with them whenever you are guided to do so. For chakra work, choose crystals associated with each of the chakras. Place the crystals on the corresponding chakra while you are lying flat. Breathe in deeply and exhale several times as you visualize your chakras being cleared and balanced.

My favorite crystals for this purpose include:

1. Root (Red) - Smoky Quartz
Dissipates negativity. Balances energies of mind and body. Protective and grounding.

2. Sacral (Orange) - Carnelian Agate
Perception, precision. Increases physical energy. Protection against emotions of fear and anger.

3. Solar Plexus (Yellow) - Citrine
Enhances body's healing energy. Good for mental focus, endurance, optimism and self-esteem.

4. Heart (Green) - Aventurine
Creativity, motivation, leadership. Stone of good luck. Balances male-female energies.

5. Throat (Blue) - Blue Lace Agate
Spirituality, grace, inspiration, inner attunement.

6. Third Eye (Indigo) - Amethyst
Enhances psychic abilities. Sedative and protective. Stone of peace and strength.

7. Crown (White/Violet) - Clear Quartz
Receives, activates, stores, transmits, and amplifies energy. Brings harmony to the soul.

• 21 •
Meditations to Assist You

Quiet the mind, and the soul will speak.
~ Ma Jaya Sati Bhagavati

**Connect to the YOU within through meditation.
Clear your mind and open your heart.**

CONSCIOUSLY CREATING WITH HEIGHTENED AWARENESS MEDITATION

THIS MEDITATION IS INTENDED TO offer a means of relaxation to evoke a higher state of awareness and to release any blocks enabling the flow of creativity. Through guided visualization, I invite you to begin creating consciously.

Take a moment to just BE. For this meditation, I invite you to lie on your back spreading your arms and legs outward. Close your eyes. Relax. Breathe in deeply and exhale.

Keep your mind calm and relaxed as you continue to be mindful of your breath. As your physical body remains motionless, focus your mind on the tips of your toes and then slowly move your awareness to each individual toe. Focus your mind on the soles of your feet, then on the tops of the feet and ankles. Become conscious of any physical feelings you experience as your mind moves from one part of your foot to another.

Move your awareness upward to your lower legs. Focus intensely on your lower legs, becoming aware of any sensations that you feel there. Become aware of the muscles and bones in your lower legs. Continue to move your mind upward to the knees, then to the thighs. Use your mind to relax the muscles in your thighs.

Focus your awareness on the pelvic region. Feel how your body is pressing down into the floor in this area. Move your awareness around the pelvic bones and the lower abdomen. Then become aware of the entire abdominal area. Soften and relax your abdomen. Move your consciousness around from the pelvic bones up toward the bottom of the rib cage.

Gently move your awareness to the lower back. Become aware of any sensations, which you may feel there. Then move your consciousness upward again to the middle back, and then to the upper back. Bring your awareness up to the shoulders.

Move your mind slowly downward along your upper arms, to your elbows and then to your lower arms. Relax your arms. Become aware of the wrists, then the palms and the backs of the hands. Move your awareness to your fingers, then to the tips of the fingers.

Focus on each individual finger separately in your mind. When you're done, move your awareness back up your arms to your shoulders.

Become aware of your neck and throat. Move your

awareness upward to the jaw, the mouth, the cheeks, the eyes, the temples, the forehead, and then up to the top of the head. Allow your consciousness to remain at the crown of the head.

Now, imagine yourself in the most beautiful tranquil place. This is your safe haven, your nirvana, your paradise. Your senses are heightened as you conceptualize this utopia.

Breathe in deeply and exhale as you begin to envision the seasons of winter, spring, summer, and fall. Allow your mind to effortlessly and easily take you from one cycle to the next.

Begin by imagining yourself in a winter wonderland. Walking in the gently fallen snow, you discover a frozen pond and reminisce of days gone by. Bundled warmly, yet feeling the coolness on your face, you turn upwards as the snowflakes continue to fall and glisten in the sunlight. Smile and relish in this moment as you embrace the feelings of winter — the taste of hot chocolate, the feeling of making snow angels, relaxing by the fireplace and hearing the embers crackle, and enjoying the taste of delicious warm apple cider.

As you transition into spring, visualize yourself traipsing through a field of green grass and wildflowers. Their fragrant smell fills your lungs as you continue to breathe in nature. The blue sky is above you and meadow continues as far as you can see. The trees' foliage is expanding before your eyes and peacefulness greets your be-ing tenderly. Smile and relish in this moment as you embrace the feelings of spring – seeing the trees bud and flourish, hearing the birds sing their individual songs, the awakening of the flowers, and the signs of life and renewal from the dormant winter.

Summer arrives and you are walking on the beach at the ocean. You feel the warmth of the sun on your skin and the sand between your toes. The waves of the ocean gently and rhythmically make their way to shore. The salt air heightens your senses as you savor the sights and sounds that surround you. As you continue to walk along the beach, smile and relish in this moment as you embrace the feelings of summer—the warmth of the sun, the smell of fresh cut grass, cookouts with your family, and sounds of children at play.

The arrival of fall is upon us. Hiking through the woods on a well-worn and familiar path, you are connecting with Mother Earth and all of her offerings. The trees' foliage is lush, providing shade and coolness as you embark on your journey. The sounds of nature are comforting and uplifting. As you continue on your way, smile and relish in this moment as you embrace the feelings of fall—leaves changing colors and dancing in the air as they escape their branches, bonfires with roasted marshmallows, and the brisk evening air.

Continue to be mindful of your breath. Feel your chest expand with the inhalations. Feel your chest deflate with the exhalations. Feel the love you have within you. Allow the essence of you to unfold and surround you.

This beautiful Divine energy surrounds your being. Allow it to envelop you fully. Open your heart to love. Be thankful for this moment and every moment. Allow this gratitude and love to flow freely through you and around you as you simply breathe.

Affirm ~ My heart overflows with gratitude and joy. I am conscious of being present in this moment. I recognize that I am a creator, and I am creating my reality. I am allowing myself to simply breathe. I am surrendering to the Universe anything and anyone that no longer serves me or my Higher purpose. I am releasing it now fully and completely. I choose to create my life and all of its experiences consciously.

Now, allow all of your desires, dreams, aspirations and intentions to fill your conscious mind. Your spirit is speaking. What does it say? Bask in the emotions you are feeling at this moment. Visualize yourself receiving and achieving all that you desire. Know that you are worthy to create the reality that you desire.

Once again, bring your consciousness to the top of the head. Move your awareness downward to the forehead, the temples, the eyes, the cheeks, the mouth, and to the jaw. Become aware of your neck and throat.

Bring your awareness down to your shoulders. Relax your arms. Move your mind slowly downward along your upper arms, to your elbows and then to your lower arms. Become aware of the wrists, then the palms and the backs of the hands. Focus on each individual finger separately in your mind. Move your awareness to your fingers, then to the tips of the fingers.

Bring your awareness back to the shoulder area. Then move your consciousness to the upper back, and then the middle back. Become aware of any sensations, which you feel there. Move your awareness to the lower back.

Move your consciousness from the bottom of the rib cage downward to the pelvic bones. Soften and relax your abdomen as you become aware once again of the entire abdominal area. Move your awareness around the pelvic bones and the lower abdomen. Feel how your body is pressing down into the floor in this area. Focus your awareness on the pelvic region.

Use your mind to relax the muscles in your thighs. Continue to move your mind down the thighs, then to the knees. Become aware of the muscles and bones in your lower legs. Focus intensely on your lower legs, becoming aware of any sensations that you feel there. Move your awareness downward to your lower legs.

Become conscious of any physical feelings you experience as your mind moves from one part of your foot to another. Focus your mind on the soles of your feet, then on the tops of the feet and ankles. Focus your mind on the tips of your toes and then slowly move your awareness to each individual toe. Keep your mind calm and relaxed as your physical body continues to be motionless, and you are mindful of your breath.

Express your gratitude for this opportunity to acknowledge your dreams and desires. Once again, be mindful of your breath. Move your fingers and wiggle your toes as you open your eyes. Choose to create consciously and creatively. Know that you are love and you are loved. And so it is.

Nowhere can man find a quieter or more untroubled retreat than in his own soul. ~ Marcus Aurelius

The following meditations have been previously included in *Connect to the YOU Within*.

∞

CONNECTING TO YOU MEDITATION

This meditation is intended to assist you in connecting with your Higher self as well as with your angels and guides.

Take a moment to just BE. Sit in a chair with your back straight and your palms up, open to receiving. Close your eyes. Relax. Breathe in deeply and exhale.

Imagine yourself in the most beautiful, tranquil place. This is your safe haven, your nirvana, your paradise. Your senses are heightened as you conceptualize this utopia.

You may be wandering in a lush green pasture of tall grass blowing gently in the wind. The smell of earth and nature fills your lungs. The blue sky is above you and there are rolling hills in the distance beckoning you. As you continue to wander, it is time to ground your energy.

Envision tree roots coming up through your feet and a vine wrapping around your legs. This vine is extending upwards into your Root Chakra, moving up into your Sacral Chakra, moving up and extending into your Solar Plexus Chakra and resting in your Heart Chakra grounding you in Mother Earth. Now, envision white light from Source consciousness coming in through your Crown Chakra, down into your Third Eye Chakra, downwards into your Throat Chakra, and meeting with Mother Earth energy at your Heart Chakra. You are grounded to earth and to Light.

Be mindful of your breath. Feel your chest expand with the inhalations. Feel your chest deflate with the exhalations. Feel the love you have within you. Allow the essence of you to unfold and surround you.

This beautiful Divine energy surrounds your being. Allow it to envelop you fully. Open your heart to love. Be thankful for this moment and every moment. Allow this gratitude and love to flow freely through you and around you as you simply breathe.

Affirm ~ My heart overflows with gratitude and joy. I am conscious of being present in this moment. I recognize the guidance I will be receiving. I am allowing myself to simply breathe. I acknowledge and appreciate that I am not alone, or my angels and guides are with me always.

Now, pay attention to the guidance you are receiving. This guidance may be from your Higher Self, your angels, and your guides. There is no need to determine the source. Simply receive and listen.

Express your gratitude for receiving the guidance you have received. Once again, be mindful of your breath. Move your fingers and wiggle your toes as you open your eyes. Know that you are love and you are loved. Remember, you are not alone on this journey. All of the answers that you seek can be found within if you take the time to listen.

Meditate. Live purely. Be quiet. Do your work with mastery. Like the moon, come out from behind the clouds! Shine. ~ Buddha

∞

AWARENESS MEDITATION

This meditation is intended to assist you in heightening your awareness.

Take a moment to just BE. Sit in a chair with your back straight and your palms up, open to receiving. Close your eyes. Relax. Breathe in deeply and exhale.

Imagine yourself in the most beautiful, tranquil place. This is your safe haven, your nirvana, your paradise. Your senses are heightened as you conceptualize this utopia.

You may be traipsing through a field of wildflowers. Their fragrant smell fills your lungs as you continue to breathe in nature. The blue sky is above you, and meadow continues as far as you can see. As you continue to traipse, it is time to ground your energy.

Envision tree roots coming up through your feet and a vine wrapping around your legs. This vine is extending upwards into your Root Chakra, moving up into your Sacral Chakra, moving up and extending into your Solar Plexus Chakra and resting in your Heart Chakra grounding you in Mother Earth. Now, envision white light from Source consciousness coming in through your Crown Chakra, downwards into your Third Eye Chakra, down into your Throat Chakra, and meeting with Mother Earth energy at your Heart Chakra. You are grounded to earth and to Light.

Be mindful of your breath. Feel your chest expand with the inhalations. Feel your chest deflate with the exhalations. Feel the love you have within you. Allow the essence of you to unfold and surround you.

This beautiful Divine energy surrounds your being. Allow it to envelop you fully. Open your heart to love. Be thankful for this moment and every moment. Allow this gratitude and love to flow freely through you and around you as you simply breathe.

Now, open your eyes slowly. Focus your energy on being present and in the now at this very moment. Be observant and become aware of your surroundings yet allow yourself to simply be.

What do you see?
What do you feel?
What do you hear?
What do you taste?
What do you smell?

Allow yourself to become fully aware and completely present right here right now. Do not allow your mind to wander. Become cognizant of this moment. Breathe in deeply and exhale mindfully. Feel your chest expanding as you breathe in and your chest deflating as you exhale. Feel your heart beating rhythmically as blood is coursing through your veins.

Notice what you are seeing with your eyes and hearing with your ears. Be fully present and fully aware of your surroundings. All you should feel at this moment is being present. Continue being mindful of your breathing and relax. You are present in this moment.

Express your gratitude for this opportunity to enhance your awareness. As you continue to be mindful of your breath, move your fingers and wiggle your toes. Know that you are love and you are loved. Remember that you are not alone on this journey. All of the answers that you seek can be found within if you take the time to listen.

In meditation, we witness our thoughts
without any judgment. ~ Author Unknown

∞

DISCOVERING YOU MEDITATION

This meditation is intended to assist you in discovering the truth of who you are.

Take a moment to just BE. Sit in a chair with your back straight and your palms up, open to receiving. Close your eyes. Relax. Breathe in deeply and exhale.

Imagine yourself in the most beautiful, tranquil place. This is your safe haven, your nirvana, your paradise. Your senses are heightened as you conceptualize this utopia.

You may be walking on a beach at the ocean. You feel the warmth of the sun on your skin, and the softness of the sand between your toes. The waves of the ocean gently and rhythmically make their way to shore. Salt air fills your nostrils as you savor the sights and sounds that surround you. As you continue to walk along the beach, it is time to ground your energy.

Envision tree roots coming up through your feet and a vine wrapping around your legs. This vine is extending upwards into your Root Chakra, moving up into your Sacral Chakra, moving up and extending into your Solar Plexus Chakra and resting in your Heart Chakra grounding you in Mother Earth. Now, envision white light from Source consciousness coming in through your Crown Chakra, downwards into your Third Eye Chakra, down into your Throat Chakra, and meeting with Mother Earth energy at your Heart Chakra. You are grounded to earth and to Light.

Be mindful of your breath. Feel your chest expand with the inhalations. Feel your chest deflate with the exhalations.

Feel the love you have within you. Allow the essence of you to unfold and surround you.

This beautiful Divine energy surrounds your being. Allow it to envelop you fully. Open your heart to love. Be thankful for this moment and every moment. Allow this gratitude and love to flow freely through you and around you as you simply breathe.

Now is the time to discover who you really are in this moment. Choose to live a life of purpose. The core of your purpose focuses solely on your happiness and well-being. When you come from a place of love and see everything, including yourself, through the eyes of love, love is all that will exist.

What makes your heart sing and your eyes twinkle? Reach down deep inside of you and allow yourself to see that you are perfect in every way. See past the illusions and the self-perceived imperfections and discover the real you – the essence of who you are. You are beautiful! You really are! You are a miraculous creation. There is no one else exactly like you, which makes you unique. Discover who you really are.

Breathe in deeply feeling the embodiment of who you are. Divine love is truly the only reality. Everything else is simply an illusion that our human-ness creates. Focus your energy on being the best you can possibly be. Focus your energy on seeing and believing that you are a beautiful and miraculous creation.

Allow yourself to embrace this clarity and greater knowing of who you really are. The knowledge you receive will help you to understand who you are, who you have been, and who you are becoming.

Express your gratitude for this opportunity to discover who you really are. Once again, be mindful of your breath. Move your fingers and wiggle your toes as you open your eyes. Know that you are love and you are loved. Remember that you are not alone on this journey. All of the answers that you seek can be found within if you take the time to listen.

Meditation is the breath of your soul. Just as breathing is the life of the body, meditation is the life of the soul.
~ Bhagwan Shree Rajneesh

∞

CONSCIOUSLY CREATING MEDITATION

This meditation is intended to assist you in consciously creating the life you desire.

Take a moment to just BE. Sit in a chair with your back straight and your palms up, open to receiving. Close your eyes. Relax. Breathe in deeply and exhale.

Imagine yourself in the most beautiful, tranquil place. This is your safe haven, your nirvana, your paradise. Your senses are heightened as you conceptualize this utopia.

You may have opted to imagine yourself in a winter wonderland. Walking in the gently falling snow, you discover a frozen pond and reminisce of days gone by. Bundled warmly yet feeling the coolness on your face, you turn upwards as the snowflakes continue to fall and glisten in the sunlight. As you smile and relish in this moment, it is time to ground your energy.

Envision tree roots coming up through your feet and a vine wrapping around your legs. This vine is extending upwards into your Root Chakra, moving up into your Sacral Chakra, moving up and extending into your Solar Plexus Chakra and resting in your Heart Chakra grounding you in Mother Earth. Now, envision white light from Source consciousness coming in through your Crown Chakra, down into your Third Eye Chakra, downwards into your Throat Chakra, and meeting with Mother Earth energy at your Heart Chakra. You are grounded to earth and to Light.

Be mindful of your breath. Feel your chest expand with the inhalations. Feel your chest deflate with the exhalations. Feel the love you have within you. Allow the essence of you to unfold and surround you.

This beautiful Divine energy surrounds your being. Allow it to envelop you fully. Open your heart to love. Be thankful for this moment and every moment. Allow this gratitude and love to flow freely through you and around you as you simply breathe.

Affirm ~ My heart overflows with gratitude and joy. I am conscious of being present in this moment. I recognize that I am a creator, and I am creating my reality. I am allowing myself to simply breathe. I am surrendering to the Universe anything and anyone that no longer serves me or my Higher purpose. I am releasing it now fully and completely. I choose to create my life and all of its experiences consciously.

Now, allow all of your desires, dreams, aspirations and intentions to fill your conscious mind. Bask in the emotions you are feeling at this moment. Visualize yourself receiving and achieving all that you desire. Know that you are worthy to create the reality that you desire.

Express your gratitude for this opportunity to acknowledge your dreams and desires. Once again, be mindful of your breath. Move your fingers and wiggle your toes as you open your eyes. Know that you are love and you are loved. Remember that you are not alone on this journey. All of the answers that you seek can be found within if you take the time to listen.

Meditation does not answer the questions of the mind, but it dissolves the very mind which creates many questions and confusion in our life. ~ Author Unknown

∞

AWAKENING MEDITATION

This meditation is intended to assist you in awakening to your purpose.

Take a moment to just BE. Sit in a chair with your back straight and your palms up, open to receiving. Close your eyes. Relax. Breathe in deeply and exhale.

Imagine yourself in the most beautiful, tranquil place. This is your safe haven, your nirvana, your paradise. Your senses are heightened as you conceptualize this utopia.

You may be hiking through the woods on a well-worn and familiar path. The trees' foliage is lush and green providing shade and coolness as you embark on your journey. The sounds of nature are comforting and uplifting. As you continue on your way, it is time to ground your energy.

Envision tree roots coming up through your feet and a vine wrapping around your legs. This vine is extending upwards into your Root Chakra, moving up into your Sacral Chakra, moving up and extending into your Solar Plexus Chakra and resting in your Heart Chakra grounding you in Mother Earth. Now, envision white light from Source consciousness coming in through your Crown Chakra, down into your Third Eye Chakra, downwards into your Throat Chakra, and meeting with Mother Earth energy at your Heart Chakra. You are grounded to earth and to Light.

Be mindful of your breath. Feel your chest expand with the inhalations. Feel your chest deflate with the exhalations.

Feel the love you have within you. Allow the essence of you to unfold and surround you.

This beautiful Divine energy surrounds your being. Allow it to envelop you fully. Open your heart to love. Be thankful for this moment and every moment. Allow this gratitude and love to flow freely through you and around you as you simply breathe.

Affirm ~ I recognize that I am not the same person I was yesterday nor will I be the same person tomorrow that I am today. My spirit is continually healing and growing. I recognize my power as I tap into my inner knowingness. I trust in the process as it unfolds.

Allow yourself to open to the flow of what the Universe has in store for you. Recognize that your purpose may simply be to be happy and live life joyfully without regret. The interaction you have with others plays a pivotal role. When you offer a kind word, a smile, an ear to listen, you are making a difference in the lives of others.

Now, pay attention to the guidance you are receiving at this time. This guidance may be from your Higher Self, your angels, and your guides. There is no need to determine the source. Simply receive and listen. Allow yourself to listen and to hear your purpose.

Express your gratitude for receiving the guidance you have received. Once again, be mindful of your breath. Move your fingers and wiggle your toes as you open your eyes. Know that you are love and you are loved. Remember that you are not alone on this journey. All of the answers that you seek can be found within if you take the time to listen.

Start with meditation, and things will go on growing in you – silence, serenity, blissfulness, sensitivity. And whatever comes out of meditation, try to bring it out in life. Share it, because everything shared grows fast. ~ Bhagwan Shree Rajneesh

CONSCIOUSLY CONNECTING MEDITATION

This meditation is intended to assist you in making conscious connections.

Take a moment to just BE. Sit in a chair with your back straight and your palms up, open to receiving. Close your eyes. Relax. Breathe in deeply and exhale.

Imagine yourself in the most beautiful, tranquil place. This is your safe haven, your nirvana, your paradise. Your senses are heightened as you conceptualize this utopia.

You may be climbing a mountain in order to see its breathtaking view. As you tread softly being mindful of your steps, you ascend higher. Exhilaration is building you reach the peak. Standing in awe of the sight that beholds you, it is time to ground your energy.

Envision tree roots coming up through your feet and a vine wrapping around your legs. This vine is extending upwards into your Root Chakra, moving up into your Sacral Chakra, moving up and extending into your Solar Plexus Chakra and resting in your Heart Chakra grounding you in Mother Earth. Now, envision white light from Source consciousness coming in through your Crown Chakra, down into your Third Eye Chakra, downwards into your Throat Chakra, and meeting with Mother Earth energy at your Heart Chakra. You are grounded to earth and to Light.

Be mindful of your breath. Feel your chest expand with the inhalations. Feel your chest deflate with the exhalations. Feel the love you have within you. Allow the essence of you to unfold and surround you.

This beautiful Divine energy surrounds your being. Allow it to envelop you fully. Open your heart to love. Be thankful for this moment and every moment. Allow this gratitude and love to flow freely through you and around you as you simply breathe.

Affirm ~ My heart overflows with gratitude and joy. I am conscious of being present in this moment. I recognize that people may be in my life for a reason, a season or a lifetime. I am allowing myself to simply breathe. I acknowledge and appreciate that when a relationship may end, it is making room for a new relationship to begin.

Sometimes, we have lingering memories that remain in our subconscious and even conscious mind. They may be of individuals or experiences we wish to release.

Allow the memory of an experience or individual you have labeled unpleasant to come into your consciousness. Do not relive the experience or try to remember the details. Simply allow this individual, event, or experience to come into your mind. Then, acknowledge and release this memory or individual you have labeled unpleasant. Say aloud, "I acknowledge. I release." Breathe in deeply and visualize yourself exhaling this experience or individual.

Continue to allow memories of an experience or individual you have labeled unpleasant to come into your mind in order for you to release them. It is imperative that you do not try to remember the details of these memories. Simply acknowledge and release them. Breathe in deeply and visualize yourself exhaling this experience or individual.

Express your gratitude for honoring all of the relationships in your life no matter the length of time. Once again, be mindful of your breath. Move your fingers and wiggle your toes as you open your eyes. Know that you are love and you are loved. Remember that you are not alone on this journey. All of the answers that you seek can be found within if you take the time to listen.

Meditation is listening to the Divine within. ~ Edgar Cayce

HONORING YOUR LIGHT MEDITATION

This meditation is intended to assist you in honoring the Light that is you and shining your Light bright.

Take a moment to just BE. Sit in a chair with your back straight and your palms up, open to receiving. Close your eyes. Relax. Breathe in deeply and exhale.

Imagine yourself in the most beautiful, tranquil place. This is your safe haven, your nirvana, your paradise. Your senses are heightened as you conceptualize this utopia.

You may be standing at the base of a waterfall surrounded by lush green foliage. The sun is peaking through the canopy of trees. Listening to the sounds of the water rush over the rocks, you feel peace, pure peace. As this feeling of peace envelops you, it is time to ground your energy.

Envision tree roots coming up through your feet and a vine wrapping around your legs. This vine is extending upwards into your Root Chakra, moving up into your Sacral Chakra, moving up and extending into your Solar Plexus Chakra and resting in your Heart Chakra grounding you in Mother Earth. Now, envision white light from Source consciousness coming in through your Crown Chakra, downwards into your Third Eye Chakra, down into your Throat Chakra, and meeting with Mother Earth energy at your Heart Chakra. You are grounded to earth and to Light.

Be mindful of your breath. Feel your chest expand with the inhalations. Feel your chest deflate with the exhalations. Feel the love you have within you. Allow the essence of you to unfold and surround you.

This beautiful Divine energy surrounds your being. Allow it to envelop you fully. Open your heart to love. Be thankful for this moment and every moment. Allow this gratitude and love to flow freely through you and around you as you simply breathe.

As you sit quietly, take a moment to perceive what your Light is and what shining your Light truly means to you. Appreciate the magnificent capacity you behold within you.

Let us now honor the Light within each one of us. Take a moment to recognize this Light as you are grounded in both Mother Earth energy and Source Consciousness energy. As you breathe in deeply and exhale, allow yourself to release anyone and anything that no longer serves you or your Higher purpose.

Affirm ~ I honor the Light within me. I honor the Light within me. I honor the Light within me. Breathe in deeply. Exhale slowly, and so it is!

Express your gratitude for your Light and its capacity to shine brightly. Honor yourself and your Light wholly and completely. Once again, be mindful of your breath. Move your fingers and wiggle your toes as you open your eyes. Know that you are love and you are loved. Remember that you are not alone on this journey. All of the answers that you seek can be found within if you take the time to listen.

Through meditation, the Higher Self is seen. ~ Bhagavad Gita

∞

OPENING YOUR HEART MEDITATION

This meditation is intended to assist you in opening your heart to love and to be loved.

Take a moment to just BE. Sit in a chair with your back straight and your palms up, open to receiving. Close your eyes. Relax. Breathe in deeply and exhale.

Imagine yourself in the most beautiful, tranquil place. This is your safe haven, your nirvana, your paradise. Your senses are heightened as you conceptualize this utopia.

You may have strolled into a hidden garden nestled behind an English cottage covered in ivy. Discovering a bench, you choose to sit down amongst the flowers and savor the sweet scents. The delicate fragrance of the roses and other flowers fill your lungs. As you sit and bask in this splendid aroma, it is time to ground your energy.

Envision tree roots coming up through your feet and a vine wrapping around your legs. This vine is extending upwards into your Root Chakra, moving up into your Sacral Chakra, moving up and extending into your Solar Plexus Chakra and resting in your Heart Chakra grounding you in Mother Earth. Now, envision white light from Source consciousness coming in through your Crown Chakra, downwards into your Third Eye Chakra, down into your Throat Chakra, and meeting with Mother Earth energy at your Heart Chakra. You are grounded to earth and to Light.

Be mindful of your breath. Feel your chest expand with the inhalations. Feel your chest deflate with the exhalations. Feel the love you have within you. Allow the essence of you to unfold and surround you.

This beautiful Divine energy surrounds your being. Allow it to envelop you fully. Open your heart to love. Be thankful for this moment and every moment. Allow this gratitude and love to flow freely through you and around you as you simply breathe.

Affirm ~ My heart overflows with gratitude and joy. I am conscious of being present in this moment. I recognize that I am love and I am loved. I am allowing myself to simply breathe.

Place one hand over your heart and feel the pulse of life within you. It is through your heart that you are connected to all things. It is here you will find your truth. Open your heart fully and freely to love and all that love beholds. Love is a nurturer of the soul. Love ignites the flame within us. Allow the love you have within you to surround you. Feel the love wash over you in waves of bliss as it cleanses your body of any pain you have previously felt.

Just as the petals of a rose opens, allow your heart to open fully. Allow yourself to receive the same love that you are sending out. Embrace and bask in this love because you are love and you are loved.

Express your gratitude for the love that is within you and surrounds you. Once again, be mindful of your breath. Move your fingers and wiggle your toes as you open your eyes. Know that you are love and you are loved. Remember that you are not alone on this journey. All of the answers that you seek can be found within if you take the time to listen.

Your love will deepen as your meditation deepens, and vice-versa: as your meditation blossoms, your love will also blossom.
~ Bhagwan Shree Rajneesh

• 22 •
Creating the Life YOU Desire

*You have been blessed with all of the energy, power and talent
you need to create the life you desire.* ~ Unknown

This is your life to live. Remember, to live it!

LIFE CHANGES HAVE BEEN OCCURRING for a lot
of people. Many are letting go of the fear and consciously
choosing to do things they have been wanting to do for a
long time. People are changing jobs, ending relationships
and moving to new locations. Having the courage to make
these life-changing choices is commendable. Remember,
you've got one "shot" as you for this lifetime. Enjoy every
moment of being YOU!

When presented with challenges, I encourage you to
pause, step back, BREATHE and then allow yourself the
opportunity to choose how you wish to react. In the big
scheme of things, there are five things you can control. You

have control of your thoughts, words, actions, emotions, and reactions. Everything else is beyond your control. You can choose how you wish to react, and sometimes the appropriate response is to have no reaction at all.

Many people allow themselves to get "sucked into the vortex" of their circumstances. I, too, allow this to happen periodically. Realistically speaking, I am sure everyone has had one experience or challenge that remains very fresh in their mind. First of all, honor your emotions in regard to what you're feeling. Secondly, is there a pattern repeating itself (same type of individual or experience or challenge presenting itself to you)? If so, the lesson for you is to acknowledge the pattern, then choose to react differently than you did before in order to break the cycle. Many times, the pattern will circle around once more just to make sure you really did see and understand the lesson.

In the big scheme of things, most experiences and challenges are pretty "small." We just perceive them to be Mt. Everest when they are really a mole hill. A visualization I often utilize with my clients is that of a surfboard on a wave. You can stand up with confidence, lie down and hold on, or let the wave come crashing down throwing you off the board altogether.

Your reaction to the challenge and its outcome is how you "ride the wave." The more you focus your energy in the present moment and trust that everything is as it should be, the easier it will be for you to make it to shore regardless of how you "rode the wave."

As I've said many times, there are two ways to view everything—through the eyes of love or through the eyes of fear. Choosing to see everyone and every experience through the eyes of love (coming from the heart space) enables you to see things from the Higher perspective—the "bigger picture!" When we view through the eyes of fear, we view experiences with worry, fear, guilt, shame, regret, frustration, anger, and feelings of lack. Like you, I have had those moments where I view experiences with fear. After all, I am human as we all are. When that happens, don't beat yourself up. We tend to be our worst critic even though we should always be our own biggest fan.

Seeing things from the Higher perspective, each one of us are expressions of Source consciousness/God. We are having this human life experience as us (who we chose to be incarnated as during this lifetime) to learn, grow, evolve, change and say what we mean to say. We truly are creating our reality with the energy we are putting out there.

The more that you allow yourself the opportunity to live in the moment by bringing all of your energy to the here and now rather than dwelling in the past or contemplating the future, the more at peace you will be. By doing so, you will also be in the flow to manifest "easier" and quicker.

∞

YOU HAVE TO ASK

I acknowledge I am someone who takes action immediately. If I say I am going to do something, I do it. I am quick to return phone calls, emails and messages even if the reply is short and to the point, saying "I'll respond to this more in depth in a few days."

Understandably, I know that people are busy and other things take priority, which is where my frustration arises. Without a doubt, this is one of my life lessons for this incarnation as Shelly Wilson. I have to recognize that not everyone is like me in this regard and that just because someone says something, it doesn't mean they will have follow through. I shouldn't take it personally. I am the only person that can make me feel discouraged or rejected (or any other emotion for that matter), so it's important to release any attachment to the outcome.

I recognize everyone is having their own human life experience. We are each unique with our own personality traits, behaviors and perception. I also know what is important to me may not be important to someone else. Therefore, sometimes we have to spell-it-out, be very clear, and ask for what we want.

This message came through loud and clear during the Healing Path Expo in December 2012 in Eureka Springs, Arkansas. I woke up Wednesday morning feeling low on energy, yet knew I needed to attend a presentation. The message I needed to hear was, "Don't assume people know what you want and can read your mind. You have to ask for what you want."

When the presenter uttered those words, my "feathers got a bit ruffled." I thought, "Seriously, I have to ask?" Then I realized my perception is different from another's. What is important to me may not be as important (or even on the radar) to someone else. Whoa... Could I do this? Would I really be able to ask for what I want? The mind chatter was chattering away — I'm not sure because I don't want people to think I have ulterior motives if I do ask nor do I wish to impose on anyone. I quickly realized people don't have a problem asking me for assistance when they need it.

∞

While working Cyndy and Tammy's Spirit Fair shortly thereafter, two very clear messages came through during the pre-fair circle. Saturday's message was "Observe, allow, let go."

I interpreted this message to mean: Observe what is going on around you with the understanding each individual is having their own human life experience.

Allow each individual to have their experience. Honor them where they are on their journey, including their beliefs. Let go of any attachment to the outcome. Let go of the need to control others. Let go of the need to appease others to simply make them happy. Make yourself happy.

The messenger continued by saying, "We are all ready to emerge out of our cocoon. No one can help you do this, or you'll wither and die because your wings aren't strong enough to support you." This made complete sense. We can ask for guidance and support from others, but ultimately it is up to us to take action and do the work ourselves.

Sunday's message was "Ask for what you want. Don't think that people already know. You have to ask." Of course, this was both validation and confirmation of the message I received a month earlier. I am definitely reaching out and asking for what I want, yet releasing any attachment to receiving a response. I know that I have to ask the question first. Then, I have a 50/50 chance of receiving the answer that I desire. Yet, if I don't ask the question, my chance is zero. This will work the same for you - be sure and ask the question.

The question may be acknowledged or ignored. The response may be yes, no, maybe or not at this time. Nonetheless, you have to ask.

∞

MANIFESTING YOUR HEART'S DESIRE

What we are today comes from our thoughts of yesterday, and our present thoughts build our life of tomorrow:
Our life is the creation of our mind. ~ Buddha

Ask and ye shall receive! The words ask and ye shall receive continue to repeat and flow within my mind. This series of seemingly simple questions are now being posed to me, thus I present them to you:

What do you desire?
What do you wish to create?
What do you wish to manifest?

The energy we exude in the form of thoughts, words and actions creates our immediate reality and affects our state of being—physically, mentally and emotionally. The intention or reasoning behind this energy plays a pivotal role in the manifestation process.

Is the intention coming from a place of love or from a place of fear?

As I've stated many times, from my perspective, there are truly two ways to view anything—through the eyes of love or through the eyes of fear. Fear comprises doubt, worry, insecurities, feelings of lack and less than. Fear resides in the lower energies, which is our human-ness or ego, and is a lower vibration. Love comes from the heart and is a higher vibration.

Recognizing that each one of us do have moments of fear and doubt as well as the other emotions, it is vitally important to honor both our lower and higher vibration emotions. In other words, acknowledge what you are feeling, and then allow yourself to express these emotions verbally, so they can be released rather than contained within our energetic be-ing.

This process begins with loving you and opening your heart to love. In doing so, you will discover your greatest gift of all—the deep connection to your Higher Self and inner knowingness. Allow your heart to open wide and let the love energy flow. Let your spirit speak and listen to what it is saying to you. Coming from a place of love will offer you the ability to see everyone and everything from the higher perspective of love recognizing that everyone is indeed having their own human life experience. In addition, it will allow you the opportunity to manifest your heart's desire from the higher vibration and intention of love rather than the lower vibration of fear and feelings of lack.

The Universal Law of Attraction is a tool for manifesting. It is based on the idea that whatever we give a lot of attention to will become part of our lives. Therefore, with every choice we make, we are co-creating with the Universe, and we are creating what will be part of our lives. What you focus on becomes your reality, so it is very important to pay attention to the energy of your thoughts, words, and actions.

In order to use the Universal Law of Attraction effectively and efficiently, it is imperative that you clearly identify what you want, focus your thoughts on what you have identified, and then allow it to manifest. In other words, do not block the manifestation from occurring by infusing it with doubt, worry, and fear. Also, take into consideration that you will attract what you desire if it is for your Highest and best good. Release the need to control the details of the manifestation process such as the how, the when, the why, the what, and the where aspects of it.

As you raise your vibration, creation seems to be happening very quickly as the Universe is working with you to bring your desires to fruition. Believe you are worthy to manifest it, visualize yourself experiencing it, allow the manifestation to happen without inhibiting the process, and you will manifest these desires if they are intended for you, meaning that what you are currently asking for doesn't interfere with the plans for learning and karmic debt repayment that you chose to work on when you were planning your current incarnation. The key word is allow. Being clear about your heart's desires while allowing the manifestation to occur is essential. Being mindful of the intention behind the manifestation should be continually acknowledged.

Remember to focus your attention on what you wish to manifest. Do NOT focus on what you already have that you don't like. You are going to manifest what you are focusing on. For example, an individual may desire money to pay bills. Many times, the energy is focused on the bills, which sends the message to the Universe that you want more bills. If you wish to increase your abundance in your life, focus on abundance and affirming that your needs are met. Expressing your gratitude for what you already have is equally important.

Be conscious of the thoughts you are having. Listen to the words that you speak and know that word modification may be necessary to avoid confusion and to be clear about your intentions. Words are energy and have their own vibration. Choose to use high-vibration words rather than low-vibration words, so that you will attract the outcome you desire. Express what you desire rather than your present state of be-ing. Be clear about what you mean. Avoid using the words trying or hoping when declaring what you want as it evokes doubt. Leave it out of the sentence completely. Use the words I am whenever possible as it is a strong declaration of what you desire.

When we are in a state of bliss and peacefulness and offering gratitude daily, these feelings and emotions flow back to us effortlessly with ease. On the other hand, when we feel sad and lonely, those feelings continue to swirl and twirl around us, leaving us in this same state. This wave of energy is assisting each one of us in rapidly manifesting what we desire.

New people are coming into our lives just as people are leaving. Chaos is coming in for some people to assist them in clearing out the clutter. However, this chaos isn't something we should fear. Rather, I encourage you to recognize it, acknowledge it, and then allow it to do its work so that you can move forward with grace and ease. It may feel painful at times, but I encourage you to see the Light through the proverbial darkness. This occurrence is making room for more Light and goodness to enter into your life. The changes may not be comfortable either, but they are necessary for continued growth.

When feeling overwhelmed during these changes, allow yourself to be mindful of your breathing - pause, inhale, and exhale. Ground and center your energy bringing your awareness to this present moment. Rather than succumbing to the thoughts that are possible, shift the energy and honor the emotions that you are feeling by acknowledging them. Then, focus your attention on raising your vibration and seeing the experiences and individuals from a higher perspective. Surrender to the Universe anything and anyone that no longer serves you or your Higher purpose, so that you may choose to create the life you desire and all of its experiences consciously.

Manifestation and creating your heart's desire occurs when you realize this and become present in the here and now. Rather than dwelling in the past or obsessively planning the future, focus on living, breathing and be-ing in the here and now. That's where creation occurs.

∞

EXERCISE TO ASSIST YOU IN CREATING YOUR HEART'S DESIRE

1. Take a moment to write down your desires, dreams, and aspirations on a piece of paper. You are worthy to receive and to achieve all that you desire. A thought becomes tangible once it is written on paper. It takes form. You can see the words and touch the paper.

2. Read what you have written and see how you feel when reading it. Release the need to know the details of the manifestation, such as how it will happen and when it will happen. Trust that all is as it should be in each and every moment.

3. Focus your attention on just one item on your list.

In doing so, you are saying, "This is what I really desire to manifest in this moment."

What is your intention for manifesting this particular desire?

Is the intention love-based or one of lack (fear-based)?

4. Envision yourself in the flow of creation. Remind yourself that you have the ability and power to create the life you desire, and most importantly, you are worthy to do so!

As Dannion Brinkley states, "You are a great, mighty and powerful spiritual being with dignity, direction and purpose!"

I am affirming that I am a great, mighty and powerful spiritual being with dignity, direction and purpose!

And so are YOU!

• Conclusion •

You must be the change you want to see in the world.
~ Mahatma Gandhi

WE MUST ALL BE THE change we wish to see in the world. Continuing to remember that we are reflections of one another, let us have the courage to be who we are without fear of judgment. Ultimately, each one of us desires to love and to be loved. Acknowledge your fellow travelers as we each embark on our own adventure called life.

Although this book is ending, my story continues because I continue to breathe. Just as my journey continues, so does yours. This journey into consciousness led me to becoming an Intuitive Medium, Reiki Master, Spiritual Teacher, and Author. My journey is not over yet because I still have work to do. Through my work and Blog Talk Radio shows, I am offering guidance and supporting others on their own journey into consciousness as well as encouraging them to live an authentic life through awareness and empowerment.

Let us continue on this journey together. My hope is you have grown from what I have shared with you, and the insight and tools I have provided for you will continue to facilitate you on your spiritual journey. In addition, I encourage you to share your journey with others because we are all teachers, just as we are students. Without even realizing the full capacity of what you behold within you, choose to share your experiences with others as you are guided to do so.

Gratefully, I wish to acknowledge five spiritual teachers who have impacted me personally: Dannion Brinkley, Sonia Choquette, John Holland, James Van Praagh, and Lisa Williams. By sharing their personal life experiences through their books, presentations and workshops, they provide tremendous wisdom and insight to each one of us. In addition, without fully realizing it, my friends and colleagues have offered me numerous educational and insightful opportunities through our conversations.

My motivation in life is to be happy and to live life fully without regret. For so many years, I simply existed. Now, I am living. I love making a difference in the lives of others. As I have stated many times before, there are two ways to view everything—through the eyes of love and through the eyes of fear. I choose to view life through the eyes of love and to assist others in doing the same.

As I reflect on my spiritual journey these past few years, my heart overflows with gratitude and joy. I am conscious of being present in this moment on this day, but I am also very excited about what I see unfolding before my eyes. I see the direction my work is going, yet I am not controlling the aspects. Rather I am allowing myself to be open to the idea of its ever evolving presence. I am taking action as I am guided, while also releasing attachment to the outcome. I trust that everything is happening in Divine time.

I recognize and am listening to the guidance I am receiving. I am acutely aware of the changes I am experiencing. I acknowledge those individuals who are coming into my life, knowing that these relationships are Divinely orchestrated. I am allowing myself to heal from old wounds that have surfaced and are no longer buried deep within me. I made the decision to shift my perception of the self-perceived unpleasant experiences and have chosen to view them instead as opportunities for learning and growth.

Most of all, I am allowing myself to simply breathe.

• Appendix •

In a series of articles for OMTimes.com, I posed the following five questions to several of my colleagues. It seems appropriate to conclude this book with my own responses to these questions as well as those responses from a few of my colleagues.

∞

JOURNEY INTO CONSCIOUSNESS
with Shelly Wilson

1. Who are you?
I know that I am a woman, a wife, a mother, a daughter, a sister, a friend - but who am I really? I am all of these and also none of these. The truth of who I really am is that I am a soul in a physical body having a human experience because my soul chose to be incarnated on Earth at this time.

I could go on to describe my physical body with height,

weight, eye color and hair color, but these are simply descriptions that will identify me. My likes and dislikes just happen to be my personal preferences. I am a soul having physical, emotional, and mental experiences. The experiences I have had are just experiences. They do not define me nor will I allow them to. The memories of these experiences comprise the totality of my life as of this moment. As I continue to live my life, more of these experiences will continue to unfold and become a part of my story, yet will not define me. I am at the center of my consciousness. I am aware that my perception — through my thoughts, emotions, and senses — creates who I am.

2. Why are you here?

I am here to acknowledge that we are all one — derived from Source energy. We are truly reflections of one another. I believe that I am here to shine my Light on others, so others can see the truth of who they really are, while encouraging them to shine their own Lights bright. Through my words and actions, I am meant to heal hearts one by one by one and see people differently than they see themselves. I believe that there are two ways to view everything — through the eyes of love and through the eyes of fear. I choose to view life through the eyes of love and to assist others in doing the same.

3. What are you supposed to be doing?

As I reflect on my spiritual journey these past few years, my heart overflows with gratitude and joy. I am conscious of being present in this moment on this day, but I am also very excited as to what I see unfolding before my eyes. I see the direction my work is going. I am not controlling the aspects, but I am allowing myself to be open to the idea of its ever evolving presence. In other words, I am not supposed to be doing anything. I am focused on simply be-ing and allowing myself to open to the flow and the realm of possibilities that anything and everything is possible. All we have to do is simply believe.

4. Do you believe that this is all there is?

I distinctly remember analyzing as a child the miracle of how I could be alive. I am breathing. My heart is beating, and blood is flowing through my veins. How is all of this even possible?

I acknowledge our reality is created by our thoughts, words and actions. If we desire something different, we are the ones who choose to change, and then, we allow the change to occur rather than resisting or inhibiting it. I am Shelly for this incarnation; yet my soul will continue once I cease to breathe.

The Spirit realm, also known as the Other Side, is literally right here all around us. Our loved ones no longer have a physical body and are vibrating at a higher frequency than the earthly plane.

5. What advice do you have for others on their journey into consciousness?

• Be present in this moment, right here right now. The past is in the past and cannot be changed. The future is yet to exist. All you have is this moment.

• Allow yourself the opportunity to recognize you are a spiritual being having a human life experience. These experiences may involve challenges as well as triumphs. Nonetheless, they are opportunities for learning and growth.

• Choose to communicate your needs and desires to yourself and to others. This is your reality. You've got one "shot" during this lifetime as YOU. Enjoy it and have no regrets.

• In addition, make sure that you tell everyone exactly how you feel. Leave no words unspoken.

• Finally, know that you are having your own human

life experience. Do not compare your journey to another's journey nor try to control someone else's journey.

• Honor yourself and what you are feeling at all times.

• Don't be afraid to ask for help and remember to love yourself always and in all ways.

∞

JOURNEY INTO CONSCIOUSNESS
with Sherri Cortland, ND

1. Who are you?

It's interesting you're asking me this question at this particular time, Shelly. In my new book, *Spiritual Toolbox*, my Guide Group channeled information about who we are that quite honestly surprised me, and I had a hard time with it at first. According to the "GG," we are all sparks of the Source/Creator/God, which isn't really news. We've all heard this before. It's what they channeled about what we're doing here that was so surprising to me. To answer your question properly, like you and everyone else on this planet, I'm a soul that is a spark of the Source who is temporarily inhabiting a human body to learn, grow, and help our species evolve.

2. Why are you here?

My primary mission is the same as all Lightworkers— to create positive energy that will help the human race continue to raise its vibratory level and therefore, continue to evolve. My secondary mission is to help others remember who they are, how powerful they are, and to help them expedite their spiritual growth. I believe that part of our spiritual growth is opening a line of direct communication with Spirit.

My mantra is everyone deserves direct communication

with Spirit.

3. What are you supposed to be doing?

I'm doing what I can to help folks establish direct communication with Spirit. I write books for Ozark Mountain Publishing, a twice-weekly metaphysical column for Examiner.com, monthly articles for *The Eden Magazine* and *Lightworkers World*, and facilitate workshops. However, I think my most important job is to smile and produce positive energy as well as show others how to do the same thing. I know this sounds elementary and maybe even silly, but a single smile is extremely contagious and spreads positive energy faster than any other thing I can think of. Through my books, I'm also charged with channeling information from Spirit to help those of us in body live our lives with less drama and pain, to understand and take responsibility for our lives, and to expedite our spiritual growth. The sooner we understand who we are, and the sooner we take responsibility for this life that we've created for ourselves; the sooner we'll understand our true power as human beings and universal beings.

4. Do you believe that this is all there is?

Absolutely not! I had no intention of writing metaphysical books, but Spirit had other plans for me - it will be interesting to see what unfolds in the coming year. I'm very sure, though, that continuing to generate as much positive energy as I can, helping people understand who they are, while helping them establish direct communication with Spirit and move forward will always be part of my life plan, no matter what other projects Spirit throws my way.

5. What advice do you have for others on their journey into consciousness?

I love this question! Meditate. Meditate every day, even if it's only for five minutes. And listen for and pay attention to that little voice within—that's the voice of your Higher Self, your inner GPS system, who wants to help you make the best choices possible to fulfill your goals. The easiest and best way to begin a journey into consciousness is to look within, and meditation is the key to unlocking who we are and what we're here to accomplish.

More about Sherri ~

Sherri Cortland, ND is the author of three metaphysical books, *Windows of Opportunity*, *Raising Our Vibrations for the New Age*, and *Spiritual Toolbox*. She also writes columns and articles for Examiner.com, *The Eden Magazine* and *Lightworker World Magazine,* and facilitates workshops on such topics as automatic writing, expediting spiritual growth, making direct contact with Spirit, and chakra balancing. Sherri lives in Orlando, FL with her husband, Ted Dylewski.

Contact Sherri at SherriCortland.com

∞

JOURNEY INTO CONSCIOUSNESS
with Jackie L. Robinson

1. Who are you?

How does one define who we are? There are labels we each wear, in which case, I am mother, sister, wife, child, friend, aunt. I am businesswoman, home manager, humanitarian, soul companion. I am a writer who loves the way words move through me and, in fact, move me. I am a proud mother to three amazing children and wife to a man with whom I'm falling in love with all over again. In the language of archetypes, I am an intellectual, queen, mystic and goddess. At the core of my being, I am Divine; a seeker of the beauty and sacred in this Earth school. I am a woman still learning to embrace all she's been given to own in this world, understanding her true power, and honoring the contract I agreed to prior to incarnating. I am a Divine being, capable of creating the life I desire, uplifting and healing myself, others, and our planet and inspiring those around me to do the same. I long for communion with the sacred, to feel it in the very center of my being. I am human too, prone to moments of unconscious emotion, overcome with frustration or heartbreak, or even fits of uncontrollable laughter. And as a human being, I allow myself to take pleasure in each delight offered me as I walk this planet— from chocolate, to kissing my husband, to a hot bath, to watching my kids be happy, to enjoying a delicious meal whether cooked by me or someone else. I am Jackie. And that's been my journey, especially as I become more and more conscious to honor and allow all that means. I am nothing and everything all at once. I most love the statement in Step 1 of 'the Steps' by Fay Hart: *I admit to myself that I am powerful beyond measure and have all I need to create the life I desire.* This is who I am.

2. Why are you here?

I came here to bring the message of love, openness, healing; to serve as chalice for all the Universe asks of me; to remain fluid as my life changes and takes on new shape throughout the years. I am a servant of the sacred. Simply stated, I came here to be Jackie.

3. What are you supposed to be doing?

Listening to the guidance of my heart and following it—living each moment as though THAT moment is my purpose. I believe our 'soul purpose' changes form as we move through life, but at its core, we are all here to love and honor ourselves and our planet while giving the best I have to give to whatever lies before me. This is my calling.

4. Do you believe that this is all there is?

I believe we are part of an infinite Universe. Our human mind can't begin to understand 'All There Is,' and yet if we quiet long enough to feel it, our soul will validate there is a greater Presence of which we are part. We are the drop in the ocean — both the drop and the ocean all at once. There is so much beyond what we can ever comprehend, of this I am certain.

5. What advice do you have for others on their journey into consciousness?

• Be gentle with yourself; there's no hurry, only a step at a time on this journey.

• You are always exactly where you're supposed to be.

• Find a teacher you trust and believe in, and let yourself be wholly seen in their presence.

• Open to new ways of seeing yourself and your life.

• Take time to sort out what you truly believe, for that will carry you through some of life's greatest challenges.

• Listen to your heart; she will always give you the best possible 'next step' for you.

• Allow yourself time to connect with your own inner truth, letting go of what you believe you're supposed to be — or be doing.

• Trust in who you are as a Divine being. THIS is your truth. Seek ways to connect to that truth in your own space and time.

• Reach out to those around you. As you grow and move through your journey, you'll attract like-minded people who will be happy to honor and support you.

• Try new things — you can never fail; only learn something new about yourself through each experience.

- Acknowledge your fear; it will lead you into new possibilities when you recognize it as a friend rather than foe.
- Remember—when you finally 'arrive'—that's when you've completed your journey and this lifetime. There's always growth and healing to be received. Open to it, feeling yourself become more and more whole as you do. I can't say it enough: trust in who you are—Divine. You came here because you chose to, with a mission and purpose to carry out as a human being. Surrender into that truth and trust it to hold and carry you through anything Life sends your way. You have a contribution that will benefit yourself and the whole. That's the journey. Enjoy the ride, my friend.

More about Jackie ~

Jackie L. Robinson is a powerful feminine force of empowerment. The last 22 years have been joyfully committed to serving as wife to an incredibly supportive husband, homemaker, and mother to three phenomenal young adults. As her family matures and her children move out into the world on their own, Jackie has found herself in transition over the last several years. She is committed to living authentically and embracing all aspects of herself. Allowing each step to guide her to the next, Jackie lives in the moment and moves with the voice of her inner passion.

You can connect with her and read her exquisitely refined soul writing on her website 'Heart Whispers' at JackieLRobinson.com.

JOURNEY INTO CONSCIOUSNESS
with Garnet Schulhauser

1. Who are you?

I am an eternal soul who will exist forever. I was created by the Source, and I remain a part of the Source. I am a being of energy that spun out from the Source like a spark of light from the Central Sun.

2. Why are you here?

I incarnated into my human body by my own choice, so I could learn and experience things on Earth necessary for my evolution as a soul. I chose the significant circumstances of my life before I was born when I developed my Life Plan. I have lived many lives on Earth before this one, and I can reincarnate as often as I desire.

3. What are you supposed to be doing?

I am supposed to be following my Life Plan. Since I don't remember what I put in my Life Plan and because I have free will to make decisions and take actions, I know that I have often strayed off course—and I will likely continue to do so in the future. I know that my spirit guides are constantly sending me guidance to steer me down the right path, but I do not always hear or understand their messages. I know that these messages are very subtle - intuitive thoughts, whispers in my mind, gut feelings, and coincidental events—and I must be diligent to quiet my mind so I can hear them.

4. Do you believe that this is all there is?

Absolutely not. This life is just a journey on Earth in a human body. When my physical body dies, I will cross over to the Spirit Side to be reunited with all of my loved ones who have crossed over before me. Once back on the Spirit Side, I will continue my evolution as a soul as I plan my next adventure.

5. What advice do you have for others on their journey into consciousness?

• Quiet your mind and listen to the messages from your guides.

• Cast aside all of your negative emotions - guilt, fear, anger, hate, and jealousy - and embrace love, compassion, and forgiveness for all other humans and creatures on Earth.

• Above all, you need to lighten up and enjoy the ride. Do not take everything so seriously.

• You cannot go wrong or become lost. Regardless of what you do in this life, you will end up back on the Spirit Side to live another day. Look at your life as an exciting adventure and relish the experience. Keep a smile on your face and laugh freely every chance you get because laughter will bring joy to your life and spread cheer to everyone around you.

More about Garnet ~

Garnet Schulhauser practiced corporate law with two large law firms in Calgary, Canada for 34 years before retiring. He is the author of *Dancing on a Stamp*

Contact Garnet at DancingonaStamp.com

JOURNEY INTO CONSCIOUSNESS
with Lloyd Matthew Thompson

1. Who are you?

My favorite way to answer this question is: This portion of my multidimensional consciousness currently resides within a physical human body many refer to as Lloyd Matthew Thompson.

That pretty much sums it up—this is not the first time I've been here, it may or may not be the last time I am here, and I am not currently ONLY here.

And neither are you!

2. Why are you here?

My Heart and Higher Self tell me I am not in this personality at this time by accident. This has been—and is—a very important pivotal point in this location of the Universe. Even the tiniest ember makes a difference in the darkness.

3. What are you supposed to be doing?

Loving.

And healing.

But healing is Loving, and Loving is healing, so…

And I'm to be writing. Maybe I'll write some books— oh wait… (I have!)

4. Do you believe that this is all there is?

Yes.

Didn't expect that answer?

I believe—and have seen—that all things on all levels are irreversibly interconnected. You cannot separate anyone or anything from anyone or anything else. And so yes, this is all there is, because all there is is ONE.

But if you mean "Is this physical reality all there is," then no, this is only a microscopic sliver of the spectrum we see here. This is only a playground — the reflection of what is REALLY going on "behind the scenes."

5. What advice do you have for others on their journey into consciousness?

Relax.

Nothing will shut you down and clam you up quicker than worry, fear, doubt, guilt, attachment, anger, and hatred. As I stated above, this place is only a playground — don't take it so seriously, but don't take it so lightly either!

Know that what you think, say, and do here very much matters, and very much shapes your own personal reality... but also know that there is no "wrong" way, or "too slow" way. Find the balance, the middle ground... but don't worry and fret about finding THAT, either. Let go.

Nothing you can do will ever mess anything up. This Universe has resources beyond our ability to even imagine — nothing is ever, ever, ever "screwed up."

What happens is simply what happens.

Go with the flow of it, whether it is something coming, something staying, or something going.

Allow no one to make you feel "bad" about anything — there is no one and nothing that will ever "punish" you, and you have no reason to feel guilty or apologize for your existence or your learning process.

So relax.

You are a magnificent piece of perfection.

More about Lloyd ~

Lloyd Matthew Thompson was raised in a strict religious household, the oldest of nine children. He has since explored, experienced, and been shaped by many other pathways, including Buddhism, Shamanism, Paganism, and New Age. Whether writing, painting, drawing or teaching, reflections of all these can be found in his work.

He has written for various metaphysical and holistic blogs and magazines, both locally and globally. He is the author of *The Galaxy Healer's Guide* and *Lightworker: A Call to Authenticity*, and is presently working on a full-length novel entitled *The Healer*, as well as the continuation of his fiction series based on the chakras entitled *The Energy Anthology*—of which the first three books, *Root*, *Sacral*, and *Solar* are now available.

Lloyd is also the healer at galaxy.energy, and the creator of the metaphysical publishing house, Starfield Press. He currently lives in Oklahoma City, Oklahoma, with his wife, triplets, daughter who thinks she is a cat, and cat who thinks she is a daughter.

www.GalaxyEnergy.org
www.StarfieldPress.com
www.the1978one.com

• Personal Recommendations •

WEBSITES

Dannion Brinkley	www.Dannion.com
Sonia Choquette	www.SoniaChoquette.com
Sherri Cortland	www.SherriCortland.com
Anthony Hidalgo	www.AnthonyHidalgo.com
John Holland	www.JohnHolland.com
ICRT	www.Reiki.org
Robinette Meyer	www.RobinetteMeyer.com
Intuitive Messenger Mitchell	www.IntuitiveMessenger.org
OMTimes Magazine	www.OMTimes.com
Ozark Mountain Publishing	www.OzarkMT.com
Helen Reddy	www.HelenReddy.com
Jackie L. Robinson	www.JackieLRobinson.com
Garnet Schulhauser	www.DancingonaStamp.com
Spirit Fair	www.SpiritFair.com
Starfield Press	www.StarfieldPress.com
Lloyd Matthew Thompson	www.GalaxyEnergy.org
James Van Praagh	www.VanPraagh.com
Lisa Williams	www.LisaWilliams.com
Shelly Wilson	www.ShellyRWilson.com

RECOMMENDED READS

The following books have assisted me on my own journey.

Quick Reference Books
Animal-Speak Pocket Guide by Ted Andrews
The Crystal Bible: A Definitive Guide to Crystals
    by Judy Hall
Heal Your Body by Louise L. Hay
The Pocket Book of Stones by Robert Simmons
Angel Numbers 101 by Doreen Virtue

Spiritual Self-Discovery Books
What If...An Exploration in Spirituality
    by Bonnie M. Cardinal
The Seven Spiritual Laws of Success by Deepak Chopra
Diary of a Psychic: Shattering the Myths
    by Sonia Choquette
Ask Your Guides by Sonia Choquette
The Time Has Come to Accept Your Intuitive Gifts!
    by Sonia Choquette
Windows of Opportunity by Sherri Cortland
Raising Our Vibrations for the New Age
    by Sherri Cortland
Spiritual Toolbox by Sherri Cortland
Awakening to your Creation by Julia Hanson
Heal Your Life by Louise L. Hay
Orbs: Their Mission and Messages of Hope
    by Klaus Heinemann, Ph.D. & Gundi Heinemann
The Spirit Whisperer by John Holland
A Spiritual Evolution by Nikki Pattillo
Dancing on a Stamp by Garnet Schulhauser
The Untethered Soul: The Journey Beyond Yourself
    by Michael A. Singer
Lightworker: A Call to Authenticity
    by Lloyd Matthew Thompson

The Galaxy Healer's Guide by Lloyd Matthew Thompson
The Lightworker's Way by Doreen Virtue
Crystal Therapy by Doreen Virtue
The Angel Therapy Handbook by Doreen Virtue
Bright Light by Dee Wallace

Spiritual Grief / Awareness of Afterlife Books
Loving Gifts from Heaven by Mary Shannon Bell
Secrets of the Light by Dannion Brinkley
Saved by the Light by Dannion Brinkley
*Bridges to Heaven: True Stores of Loved Ones
    on the Other Side* by Sue Frederick
Transitions: A Nurse's Education about Life and Death
    by Becki Hawkins
Talking to Heaven by James Van Praagh
Heaven and Earth by James Van Praagh
Survival of the Soul by Lisa Williams

Living Life Books
The Last Lecture by Randy Pausch with Jeffrey Zaslow
How Full is Your Bucket?
    by Tom Rath and Donald O. Clifton

Divination Tools
The Answer is Simple Oracle Cards by Sonia Choquette
Divine Guidance by Cheryl Lee Harnish
Path of the Soul Destiny Cards by Cheryl Lee Harnish
Return of Spirit by Cheryl Lee Harnish
Soul Coaching Oracle Cards by Denise Linn
Healing with the Angels Oracle Cards by Doreen Virtue
Angel Therapy Oracle Cards by Doreen Virtue
Archangel Oracle Cards by Doreen Virtue
PsyCards by U.S Games Systems, Inc.

• About Shelly •

INTUITIVE MEDIUM, REIKI MASTER, and Spiritual Teacher Shelly Wilson would love to assist you on your spiritual journey. With respect, truth, integrity, and love, Shelly honors your free will and recognizes that you are co-creating your reality with the Universe. She offers private readings, intuitive coaching, Reiki sessions, and teaches workshops. Shelly's books, *28 Days to a New YOU* and *Connect to the YOU Within*, are available in paperback and all electronic formats. Her courses, *Stop Existing and Start Living!* and *Opening Your Heart to Love* are available through the DailyOM. In addition, Shelly is the host of *The Shelly Wilson Show* and *Journey into Consciousness* on Blog Talk Radio.

www.ShellyRWilson.com
www.Journey-into-Consciousness.com
www.facebook.com/IntuitiveMediumShelly
www.facebook.com/JourneyintoConsciousness
www.blogtalkradio.com/ShellyWilson
www.blogtalkradio.com/JourneyintoConsciousness

8378969R00164

Made in the USA
San Bernardino, CA
07 February 2014